The History of Xerxes

The History of Xerxes

Makers of History Series

Jacob Abbott

Cedar Lake Classics

Copyright © 2023 by Cedar Lake Classics

This is an annotated edition of a public domain work.

CONTENTS

PHOTO INSERT vii
PREFACE ix

1. The Mother of Xerxes 1
2. Egypt and Greece 13
3. Debate on the Proposed Invasion of Greece 26
4. Preparations for the Invasion of Greece 39
5. Crossing the Hellsepont 52
6. The Review of the Troops at Doriscus 65
7. The Preparations of the Greeks for Defense 81
8. The Advance of Xerxes into Greece 96
9. The Battle of Thermopylæ 110
10. The Burning of Athens 124
11. The Battle of Salamis 136

CONTENTS

12 | The Return of Xerxes to Persia 159

ABOUT JACOB ABBOTT 171
BIOGRAPHIES ABBOTT WROTE 173

Portrait of Xerxes.

PREFACE

ONE special object which the author of this series has had in view, in the plan and method which he has followed in the preparation of the successive volumes, has been to adapt them to the purposes of text-books in schools. The study of a _general compend_ of history, such as is frequently used as a text-book, is highly useful, if it comes in at the right stage of education, when the mind is sufficiently matured, and has acquired sufficient preliminary knowledge to understand and appreciate so condensed a generalization as a summary of the whole history of a nation contained in an ordinary volume must necessarily be. Without this degree of maturity of mind, and this preparation, the study of such a work will be, as it too frequently is, a mere mechanical committing to memory of names, and dates, and phrases, which awaken no interest, communicate no ideas, and impart no useful knowledge to the mind.

A class of ordinary pupils, who have not yet become much acquainted with history, would, accordingly, be more benefited by having their attention concentrated, at first, on detached and separate topics, such as those which form the subjects, respectively, of these volumes. By studying thus fully the history of individual monarchs, or the narratives of single events, they can go more fully into detail; they conceive of the transactions described as realities; their reflecting and reasoning powers are occupied on what they read; they take notice of the motives of conduct, of the gradual development of character, the good or ill desert of actions, and of the connection of causes and consequences, both in respect to the influence of wisdom and virtue on the one hand, and, on the other, of folly and crime. In a word, their _minds_ and _hearts_ are occupied instead of merely their memories. They reason, they

PREFACE

sympathize, they pity, they approve, and they condemn. They enjoy the real and true pleasure which constitutes the charm of historical study for minds that are mature; and they acquire a taste for truth instead of fiction, which will tend to direct their reading into proper channels in all future years.

The use of these works, therefore, as text-books in classes, has been kept continually in mind in the preparation of them. The running index on the tops of the pages is intended to serve instead of questions. These captions can be used in their present form as _topics_, in respect to which, when announced in the class, the pupils are to repeat substantially what is said on the page; or, on the other hand, questions in form, if that mode is preferred, can be readily framed from them by the teacher. In all the volumes, a very regular system of division is observed, which will greatly facilitate the assignment of lessons.

Map of the Persian Empire

1

The Mother of Xerxes

B.C. 522-484

Persian magnificence.—The mother of Xerxes.—Cambyses.—Ambition and selfishness of kings.—General influence exerted by great sovereigns upon the community.—Labors of great conquerors.—Caesar.—Darius. —William the Conqueror.—Napoleon.—Heroes and conquerors.—The main spring of their actions.—Cyrus.—Character and career of Cambyses.—Wives of Cambyses.—He marries his sister.—Death of Cambyses.— Smerdis the magian.—Cunning of Smerdis.—His feeling of insecurity. —Smerdis suspected.—His imposture discovered.—Death of Smerdis.— Succession of Darius.—Atossa's sickness.—The Greek physician.—Atossa's promise.—Atossa's conversation with Darius.—Success of her plans.—The expedition to Greece.—Escape of the physician.—Atossa's four sons.—Artobazanes.—Dispute about the succession.—Xerxes and Artobazanes.—The arguments.—Influence of Atossa.—The Spartan fugitive.—His views of the succession.—The decision.—Death of Darius.

THE name of Xerxes is associated in the minds of men with the idea of the highest attainable elevation of human magnificence and grandeur. This monarch was the sovereign of the ancient Persian empire when it was at the height of its prosperity and power. It is probable, however, that his greatness and fame lose nothing by the manner in which his story comes down to us through the Greek historians. The Greeks conquered Xerxes, and, in relating his history, they magnify the wealth, the power, and the resources of his empire, by way of exalting the greatness and renown of their own exploits in subduing him.

The mother of Xerxes was Atossa, a daughter of Cyrus the Great, who was the founder of the Persian empire. Cyrus was killed in Scythia, a wild and barbarous region lying north of the Black and Caspian Seas. His son Cambyses succeeded him.

A kingdom, or an empire, was regarded, in ancient days, much in the light of an estate, which the sovereign held as a species of property, and which he was to manage mainly with a view to the promotion of his own personal aggrandizement and pleasure. A king or an emperor could have more palaces, more money, and more wives than other men; and if he was of an overbearing or ambitious spirit, he could march into his neighbors' territories, and after gratifying his love of adventure with various romantic exploits, and gaining great renown by his ferocious impetuosity in battle, he could end his expedition, perhaps, by adding his neighbors' palaces, and treasures, and wives to his own.

Divine Providence, however, the mysterious power that overrules all the passions and impulses of men, and brings extended and general good out of local and particular evil, has made the ambition and the selfishness of princes the great means of preserving order and government among men. These great ancient despots, for example, would not have been able to collect their revenues, or enlist their armies, or procure supplies for their campaigns, unless their dominions were under a regular and complete system of social organization, such as should allow all the industrial pursuits of commerce and of agriculture, throughout the mass of the community, to go regularly on. Thus absolute monarchs, however ambitious, and selfish, and domineering in their characters, have a strong personal interest in the establishment of order and of justice between man and man throughout all the regions which are under their sway. In fact, the greater their ambition, their selfishness, and their pride, the stronger will this interest be; for, just in proportion as order, industry, and internal tranquillity prevail in a country, just in that proportion can revenues be collected from it, and armies raised and maintained.

It is a mistake, therefore, to suppose of the great heroes, and sovereigns, and conquerors that have appeared from time to time among mankind, that the usual and ordinary result of their influence and action has been that of disturbance and disorganization. It is true that a vast amount of disturbance and disorganization has often followed from the march of their armies, their sieges, their invasions, and the other local and temporary acts of violence which they commit; but these are the exceptions, not the rule. It must be that such things are exceptions, since, in any extended and general view of the subject, a much greater amount of social organization, industry, and peace is necessary to raise and maintain an army, than that army can itself destroy. The deeds of destruction which great conquerors perform attract more attention and make a greater impression upon mankind than the quiet, patient, and long-continued labors by which they perfect and extend the general organization of the social state. But these labors, though less noticed by men, have really employed the energies of great sovereigns in a far greater degree than mankind have generally imagined. Thus we should describe the work of Caesar's life in a single word more truly by saying that he organized Europe, than that he conquered it. His bridges, his roads, his systems of jurisprudence, his coinage, his calendar, and other similar means and instruments of social arrangement, and facilities for promoting the pursuits of industry and peace, mark, far more properly, the real work which that great conqueror performed among mankind, than his battles and his victories. Darius was, in the same way, the organizer of Asia. William the Conqueror completed, or, rather, advanced very far toward completing, the social organization of England; and even in respect to Napoleon, the true and proper memorial of his career is the successful working of the institutions, the systems, and the codes which he perfected and introduced into the social state, and not the brazen column, formed from captured cannon, which stands in the Place Vendôme.

These considerations, obviously true, though not always borne in mind, are, however, to be considered as making the characters of the great sovereigns, in a moral point of view, neither the worse nor the better. In all that they did, whether in arranging and systematizing the functions of social life, or in ruthless deeds of conquest and destruction, they were actuated, in a great measure, by selfish ambition. They arranged and organized the social state in order to form a more compact and solid pedestal for the foundation of their power. They maintained peace and order among their people, just as a master would suppress quarrels among his slaves, because peace among laborers is essential to productive results. They fixed and defined legal rights, and established courts to determine and enforce them; they protected property; they counted and classified men; they opened roads; they built bridges; they encouraged commerce; they hung robbers, and exterminated pirates—all, that the collection of their revenues and the enlistment of their armies might go on without hinderance or restriction. Many of them, indeed, may have been animated, in some degree, by a higher and nobler sentiment than this. Some may have felt a sort of pride in the contemplation of a great, and prosperous, and wealthy empire, analogous to that which a proprietor feels in surveying a well-conditioned, successful, and productive estate. Others, like Alfred, may have felt a sincere and honest interest in the welfare of their fellow-men, and the promotion of human happiness may have been, in a greater or less degree, the direct object of their aim. Still, it can not be denied that a selfish and reckless ambition has been, in general, the main spring of action with heroes and conquerors, which, while it aimed only at personal aggrandizement, has been made to operate, through the peculiar mechanism of the social state which the Divine wisdom has contrived, as a means, in the main of preserving and extending peace and order among mankind, and not of destroying them.

But to return to Atossa. Her father Cyrus, who laid the foundation of the great Persian empire, was, for a hero and conqueror, tolerably considerate and just, and he desired, probably, to promote the welfare and happiness of his millions of subjects; but his son Cambyses, Atossa's brother, having been brought up in expectation of succeeding to vast wealth and power, and having been, as the sons of the wealthy and the powerful often are in all ages of the world, wholly neglected by his father during the early part of his life, and entirely unaccustomed to control, became a wild, reckless, proud, selfish, and ungovernable young man. His father was killed suddenly in battle, as has already been stated, and Cambyses succeeded him. Cambyses's career was short, desperate, and most tragical in its end. In fact, he was one of the most savage, reckless, and abominable monsters that have ever lived.

It was the custom in those days for the Persian monarchs to have many wives, and, what is still more remarkable, whenever any monarch died, his successor inherited his predecessor's family as well as his throne. Cyrus had several children by his various wives. Cambyses and Smerdis were the only sons, but there were daughters, among whom Atossa was the most distinguished. The ladies of the court were accustomed to reside in different palaces, or in different suites of apartments in the same palace, so that they lived in a great measure isolated from each other. When Cambyses came to the throne, and thus entered into possession of his father's palaces, he saw and fell in love with one of his father's daughters. He wished to make her one of his wives. He was accustomed to the unrestricted indulgence of every appetite and passion, but he seems to have had some slight misgivings in regard to such a step as this. He consulted the Persian judges. They conferred upon the subject, and then replied that they had searched among the laws of the realm, and though they found no law allowing a man to marry his sister, they found many which authorized a Persian king to do whatever he pleased.

Cambyses therefore added the princess to the number of his wives, and not long afterward he married another of his father's daughters in the same way. One of these princesses was Atossa.

Cambyses invaded Egypt, and in the course of his mad career in that country he killed his brother Smerdis and one of his sisters, and at length was killed himself. Atossa escaped the dangers of this stormy and terrible reign, and returned safely to Susa after Cambyses's death.

Smerdis, the brother of Cambyses, would have been Cambyses's successor if he had survived him; but he had been privately assassinated by Cambyses's orders, though his death had been kept profoundly secret by those who had perpetrated the deed. There was another Smerdis in Susa, the Persian capital, who was a magian—that is, a sort of priest—in whose hands, as regent, Cambyses had left the government while he was absent on his campaigns. This magian Smerdis accordingly conceived the plan of usurping the throne, as if he were Smerdis the prince, resorting to a great many ingenious and cunning schemes to conceal his deception. Among his other plans, one was to keep himself wholly sequestered from public view, with a few favorites, such, especially, as had not personally known Smerdis the prince. In the same manner he secluded from each other and from himself all who had known Smerdis, in order to prevent their conferring with one another, or communicating to each other any suspicions which they might chance to entertain. Such seclusion, so far as related to the ladies of the royal family, was not unusual after the death of a king, and Smerdis did not deviate from the ordinary custom, except to make the isolation and confinement of the princesses and queens more rigorous and strict than common. By means of this policy he was enabled to go on for some months without detection, living all the while in the greatest luxury and splendor, but at the same time in absolute seclusion, and in unceasing anxiety and fear.

One chief source of his solicitude was lest he should be detected by means of his ears! Some years before, when he was in a comparatively obscure position, he had in some way or other offended his sovereign, and was punished by having his ears cut off. It was necessary, therefore, to keep the marks of this mutilation carefully concealed by means of his hair and his head-dress, and even with these precautions he could never feel perfectly secure.

At last one of the nobles of the court, a sagacious and observing man, suspected the imposture. He had no access to Smerdis himself, but his daughter, whose name was Phaedyma, was one of Smerdis's wives. The nobleman was excluded from all direct intercourse with Smerdis, and even with his daughter; but he contrived to send word to his daughter, inquiring whether her husband was the true Smerdis or not. She replied that she did not know, inasmuch as she had never seen any other Smerdis, if, indeed, there had been another. The nobleman then attempted to communicate with Atossa, but he found it impossible to do so. Atossa had, of course, known her brother well, and was on that very account very closely secluded by the magian. As a last resort, the nobleman sent to his daughter a request that she would watch for an opportunity to feel for her husband's ears while he was asleep. He admitted that this would be a dangerous attempt, but his daughter, he said, ought to be willing to make it, since, if her pretended husband were really an impostor, she ought to take even a stronger interest than others in his detection. Phaedyma was at first afraid to undertake so dangerous a commission; but she at length ventured to do so, and, by passing her hand under his turban one night, while he was sleeping on his couch, she found that the ears were gone.

The consequence of this discovery was, that a conspiracy was formed to dethrone and destroy the usurper. The plot was successful. Smerdis was killed; his imprisoned queens were set free, and Darius was raised to the throne in his stead.

Atossa now, by that strange principle of succession which has been already alluded to, became the wife of Darius, and she figures frequently and conspicuously in history during his long and splendid reign.

Her name is brought into notice in one case in a remarkable manner, in connection with an expedition which Darius sent on an exploring tour into Greece and Italy. She was herself the means, in fact, of sending the expedition. She was sick; and after suffering secretly and in silence as long as possible—the nature of her complaint being such as to make her unwilling to speak of it to others—she at length determined to consult a Greek physician who had been brought to Persia as a captive, and had acquired great celebrity at Susa by his medical science and skill. The physician said that he would undertake her case on condition that she would promise to grant him a certain request that he would make. She wished to know what it was beforehand, but the physician would not tell her. He said, however, that it was nothing that it would be in any way derogatory to her honor to grant him.

On these conditions Atossa concluded to agree to the physician's proposals. He made her take a solemn oath that, if he cured her of her malady, she would do whatever he required of her, provided that it was consistent with honor and propriety. He then took her case under his charge, prescribed for her and attended her, and in due time she was cured. The physician then told her that what he wished her to do for him was to find some means to persuade Darius to send him home to his native land.

Atossa was faithful in fulfilling her promise. She took a private opportunity, when she was alone with Darius, to propose that he should engage in some plans of foreign conquest. She reminded him of the vastness of the military power which was at his disposal, and of the facility with which, by means of it, he might extend his dominions. She extolled, too, his genius and energy, and endeavored to inspire in his mind some ambitious desires to distinguish himself in the estimation of mankind by bringing his capacities for the performance of great deeds into action.

Darius listened to these suggestions of Atossa with interest and with evident pleasure. He said that he had been forming some such plans himself. He was going to build a bridge across the Hellespont or the Bosporus, to unite Europe and Asia; and he was also going to make an incursion into the country of the Scythians, the people by whom Cyrus, his great predecessor, had been defeated and slain. It would be a great glory for him, he said, to succeed in a conquest in which Cyrus had so totally failed.

But these plans would not answer the purpose which Atossa had in view. She urged her husband, therefore, to postpone his invasion of the Scythians till some future time, and first conquer the Greeks, and annex their territory to his dominions. The Scythians, she said, were savages, and their country not worth the cost of conquering it, while Greece would constitute a noble prize. She urged the invasion of Greece, too, rather than Scythia, as a personal favor to herself, for she had been wanting, she said, some slaves from Greece for a long time—some of the women of Sparta, of Corinth, and of Athens, of whose graces and accomplishments she had heard so much.

There was something gratifying to the military vanity of Darius in being thus requested to make an incursion to another continent, and undertake the conquest of the mightiest nation of the earth, for the purpose of procuring accomplished waiting-maids to offer as a present to his queen. He became restless and excited while listening to Atossa's proposals, and to the arguments with which she enforced them, and it was obvious that he was very strongly inclined to accede to her views. He finally concluded to send a commission into Greece to explore the country, and to bring back a report on their return; and as he decided to make the Greek physician the guide of the expedition, Atossa gained her end.

A full account of this expedition, and of the various adventures which the party met with on their voyage, is given in our history of Darius. It may be proper to say here, however, that the physician fully succeeded in his plans of making his escape. He pretended, at first, to be unwilling to go, and he made only the most temporary arrangements in respect to the conduct of his affairs while he should be gone, in order to deceive the king in regard to his intentions of not returning. The king, on his part, resorted to some stratagems to ascertain whether the physician was sincere in his professions, but he did not succeed in detecting the artifice, and so the party went away. The physician never returned.

Atossa had four sons. Xerxes was the eldest of them. He was not, however, the eldest of the sons of Darius, as there were other sons, the children of another wife, whom Darius had married before he ascended the throne. The oldest of these children was named Artobazanes. Artobazanes seems to have been a prince of an amiable and virtuous character, and not particularly ambitious and aspiring in his disposition, although, as he was the eldest son of his father, he claimed to be his heir. Atossa did not admit the validity of this claim, but maintained that the oldest of her children was entitled to the inheritance.

It became necessary to decide this question before Darius's death; for Darius, in the prosecution of a war in which he was engaged, formed the design of accompanying his army on an expedition into Greece, and, before doing this, he was bound, according to the laws and usages of the Persian realm, to regulate the succession.

There immediately arose an earnest dispute between the friends and partisans of Artobazanes and Xerxes, each side urging very eagerly the claims of its own candidate. The mother and the friends of Artobazanes maintained that he was the oldest son, and, consequently, the heir. Atossa, on the other hand, contended that Xerxes was the grandson of Cyrus, and that he derived from that circumstance the highest possible hereditary rights to the Persian throne.

This was in some respects true, for Cyrus had been the founder of the empire and the legitimate monarch, while Darius had no hereditary claims. He was originally a noble, of high rank, indeed, but not of the royal line; and he had been designated as Cyrus's successor in a time of revolution, because there was, at that time, no prince of the royal family who could take the inheritance. Those, therefore, who were disposed to insist on the claims of a legitimate hereditary succession, might very plausibly claim that Darius's government had been a regency rather than a reign; that Xerxes, being the oldest son of Atossa, Cyrus's daughter, was the true representative of the royal line; and that, although it might not be expedient to disturb the possession of Darius during his lifetime, yet that, at his death, Xerxes was unquestionably entitled to the throne.

There was obviously a great deal of truth and justice in this reasoning, and yet it was a view of the subject not likely to be very agreeable to Darius, since it seemed to deny the existence of any real and valid title to the sovereignty in him. It assigned the crown, at his death, not to his son as such, but to his predecessor's grandson; for though Xerxes was both the son of Darius and the grandson of Cyrus, it was in the latter capacity that he was regarded as entitled to the crown in the argument referred to above. The doctrine was very gratifying to the pride of Atossa, for it made Xerxes the successor to the crown as her son and heir, and not as the son and heir of her husband. For this very reason it was likely to be not very gratifying to Darius. He hesitated very much in respect to adopting it. Atossa's ascendency over his mind, and her influence generally in the Persian court, was almost overwhelming, and yet Darius was very unwilling to seem, by giving to the oldest grandson of Cyrus the precedence over his own eldest son, to admit that he himself had no legitimate and proper title to the throne.

While things were in this state, a Greek, named Demaratus, arrived at Susa. He was a dethroned prince from Sparta, and had fled from the political storms of his own country to seek refuge in Darius's capital. Demaratus found a way to reconcile Darius's pride as a sovereign with his personal preferences as a husband and a father. He told the king that, according to the principles of hereditary succession which were adopted in Greece, Xerxes was his heir as well as Cyrus's, for he was the oldest son who was born after his accession. A son, he said, according to the Greek ideas on the subject, was entitled to inherit only such rank as his father held when the son was born; and that, consequently, none of his children who had been born before his accession could have any claims to the Persian throne. Artobazanes, in a word, was to be regarded, he said, only as the son of Darius the noble, while Xerxes was the son of Darius the king.

In the end Darius adopted this view, and designated Xerxes as his successor in case he should not return from his distant expedition. He did not return. He did not even live to set out upon it. Perhaps the question of the succession had not been absolutely and finally settled, for it arose again and was discussed anew when the death of Darius occurred. The manner in which it was finally disposed of will be described in the next chapter.

2

Egypt and Greece

B.C. 484

Xerxes assumes the crown.—His message to Artobazanes.—Question of the succession again debated.—Advice of Atossa.—Decision of Artabanus.—Unfinished wars of Darius.—Egypt and Greece.—Character of the Egyptians.—Character of the Greeks.—Architecture.—Monuments of Greece.—Egyptian architecture.—Form of Egypt.—Delta of the Nile.—Fertility of Egypt.—No rain in Egypt.—Rising of the Nile.—Preparations for the inundation.—Gradual rise of the water.—Appearance of the country during an inundation.—The three theories.—Objections to the first.—Second and third theories.—Reasons against them.—Ideas of the common people in regard to the inundation.—Story of King Pheron.—His punishment.—Sequel of the story of King Pheron.—Nilometers.—Use of Nilometers.—Enormous structures of Egypt.—Comparative antiquity of various objects.—Great age of the Pyramids.—Egypt a mark for the conqueror.—Its relation to Persia.—Xerxes resolves to subdue Egypt first.—The Jews.—The Egyptians subdued.—Return to Susa.

THE arrangements which Darius had made to fix and determine the succession, before his death, did not entirely prevent the question from arising again when his death occurred. Xerxes was on the spot at the time, and at once assumed the royal functions. His brother was absent. Xerxes sent a messenger to Artobazanes informing him of their father's death, and of his intention of assuming the crown. He said, however, that if he did so, he should give his brother the second rank, making him, in all respects, next to himself in office and honor. He sent, moreover, a great many splendid presents to Artobazanes, to evince the friendly regard which he felt for him, and to propitiate his favor.

Artobazanes sent back word to Xerxes that he thanked him for his presents, and that he accepted them with pleasure. He said that he considered himself, nevertheless, as justly entitled to the crown, though he should, in the event of his accession, treat all his brothers, and especially Xerxes, with the utmost consideration and respect.

Soon after these occurrences, Artobazanes came to Media, where Xerxes was, and the question which of them should be the king was agitated anew among the nobles of the court. In the end, a public hearing of the cause was had before Artabanus, a brother of Darius, and, of course, an uncle of the contending princes. The question seems to have been referred to him, either because he held some public office which made it his duty to consider and decide such a question, or else because he had been specially commissioned to act as judge in this particular case. Xerxes was at first quite unwilling to submit his claims to the decision of such a tribunal. The crown was, as he maintained, rightfully his. He thought that the public voice was generally in his favor. Then, besides, he was already in possession of the throne, and by consenting to plead his cause before his uncle, he seemed to be virtually abandoning all this vantage ground, and trusting instead to the mere chance of Artabanus's decision.

Atossa, however, recommended to him to accede to the plan of referring the question to Artabanus. He would consider the subject, she said, with fairness and impartiality, and decide it right. She had no doubt that he would decide it in Xerxes's favor; "and if he does not," she added, "and you lose your cause, you only become the second man in the kingdom instead of the first, and the difference is not so very great, after all."

Atossa may have had some secret intimation how Artabanus would decide.

However this may be, Xerxes at length concluded to submit the question. A solemn court was held, and the case was argued in the presence of all the nobles and great officers of state. A throne was at hand to which the successful competitor was to be conducted as soon as the decision should be made. Artabanus heard the arguments, and decided in favor of Xerxes. Artobazanes, his brother, acquiesced in the decision with the utmost readiness and good humor. He was the first to bow before the king in token of homage, and conducted him, himself, to the throne.

Xerxes kept his promise faithfully of making his brother the second in his kingdom. He appointed him to a very high command in the army, and Artobazanes, on his part, served the king with great zeal and fidelity, until he was at last killed in battle, in the manner hereafter to be described.

As soon as Xerxes found himself established on his throne, he was called upon to decide immediately a great question, namely, which of two important wars in which his father had been engaged he should first undertake to prosecute, the war in Egypt or the war in Greece.

By referring to the map, the reader will see that, as the Persian empire extended westward to Asia Minor and to the coasts of the Mediterranean Sea, the great countries which bordered upon it in this direction were, on the north Greece, and on the south, Egypt; the one in Europe, and the other in Africa. The Greeks and the Egyptians were both wealthy and powerful, and the countries which they respectively inhabited were fertile and beautiful beyond expression, and yet in all their essential features and characteristics they were extremely dissimilar. Egypt was a long and narrow inland valley. Greece reposed, as it were, in the bosom of the sea, consisting, as it did, of an endless number of islands, promontories, peninsulas, and winding coasts, laved on every side by the blue waters of the Mediterranean. Egypt was a plain, diversified only by the varieties of vegetation, and by the towns and villages, and the enormous monumental structures which had been erected by man. Greece was a picturesque and ever-changing scene of mountains and valleys; of precipitous cliffs, winding beaches, rocky capes, and lofty headlands. The character and genius of the inhabitants of these two countries took their cast, in each case, from the physical conformations of the soil. The Egyptians were a quiet, gentle, and harmless race of tillers of the ground. They spent their lives in pumping water from the river, in the patient, persevering toil of sowing smooth and mellow fields, or in reaping the waving grain. The Greeks drove flocks and herds up and down the declivities of the mountains, or hunted wild beasts in forests and fastnesses. They constructed galleys for navigating the seas; they worked the mines and manufactured metals. They built bridges, citadels, temples, and towns, and sculptured statuary from marble blocks which they chiseled from the strata of the mountains. It is surprising what a difference is made in the genius and character of man by elevations, here and there, of a few thousand feet in the country where his genius and character are formed.

The architectural wonders of Egypt and of Greece were as diverse from each other as the natural features of the soil, and in each case the structures were in keeping and in harmony with the character of the landscape which they respectively adorned. The harmony was, however, that of contrast, and not of correspondence. In Greece, where the landscape itself was grand and sublime, the architect aimed only at beauty. To have aimed at magnitude and grandeur in human structures among the mountains, the cliffs, the cataracts, and the resounding ocean shores of Greece, would have been absurd. The Grecian artists were deterred by their unerring instincts from the attempt. They accordingly built beautiful temples, whose white and symmetrical colonnades adorned the declivities, or crowned the summits of the hills. They sculptured statues, to be placed on pedestals in groves and gardens; they constructed fountains; they raised bridges and aqueducts on long ranges of arches and piers; and the summits of ragged rocks crystallized, as it were, under their hands into towers, battlements, and walls. In Egypt, on the other hand, where the country itself was a level and unvarying plain, the architecture took forms of prodigious magnitude, of lofty elevation, and of vast extent. There were ranges of enormous columns, colossal statues, towering obelisks, and pyramids rising like mountains from the verdure of the plain. Thus, while nature gave to the country its elements of beauty, man completed the landscape by adding to it the grand and the sublime.

The shape and proportions of Egypt would be represented by a green ribbon an inch wide and a yard long, lying upon the ground in a serpentine form; and to complete the model, we might imagine a silver filament passing along the center of the green to denote the Nile. The real valley of verdure, however, is not of uniform breadth, like the ribbon so representing it, but widens as it approaches the sea, as if there had been originally a gulf or estuary there, which the sediment from the river had filled.

In fact, the rich and fertile plain which the alluvial deposits of the Nile have formed, has been protruded for some distance into the sea, and the stream divides itself into three great branches about a hundred miles from its mouth, two outermost of which, with the sea-coast in front, inclose a vast triangle, which was called the Delta, from the Greek letter delta, (Greek: D), which is of a triangular form. In ascending the river beyond the Delta, the fertile plain, at first twenty-five or thirty miles wide, grows gradually narrower, as the ranges of barren hills and tracts of sandy deserts on either hand draw nearer and nearer to the river. Thus the country consists of two long lines of rich and fertile intervals, one on each side of the stream. In the time of Xerxes the whole extent was densely populated, every little elevation of the land being covered with a village or a town. The inhabitants tilled the land, raising upon it vast stores of corn, much of which was floated down the river to its mouth, and taken thence to various countries of Europe and Asia, in merchant ships, over the Mediterranean Sea. Caravans, too, sometimes came across the neighboring deserts to obtain supplies of Egyptian corn. This was done by the sons of Jacob when the crops failed them in the land of Canaan, as related in the sacred Scriptures.

There were two great natural wonders in Egypt in ancient times as now: first, it never rained there, or, at least, so seldom, that rain was regarded as a marvelous phenomenon, interrupting the ordinary course of nature, like an earthquake in England or America. The falling of drops of water out of clouds in the sky was an occurrence so strange, so unaccountable, that the whole population regarded it with astonishment and awe. With the exception of these rare and wonder-exciting instances, there was no rain, no snow, no hail, no clouds in the sky. The sun was always shining, and the heavens were always serene. These meteorological characteristics of the country, resulting, as they do, from permanent natural causes, continue, of course, unchanged to the present day; and the Arabs who live now along the banks of the river, keep their crops, when harvested, in heaps in the open air, and require no roofs to their huts except a light covering of sheaves to protect the inmates from the sun.

The other natural wonder of Egypt was the annual rising of the Nile. About midsummer, the peasantry who lived along the banks would find the river gradually beginning to rise. The stream became more turbid, too, as the bosom of the waters swelled. No cause for this mysterious increase appeared, as the sky remained as blue and serene as before, and the sun, then nearly vertical, continued to shine with even more than its wonted splendor. The inhabitants however, felt no surprise, and asked for no explanation of the phenomenon. It was the common course of nature at that season. They had all witnessed it, year after year, from childhood. They, of course, looked for it when the proper month came round, and, though they would have been amazed if the annual flood had failed, they thought nothing extraordinary of its coming.

When the swelling of the waters and the gradual filling of the channels and low grounds in the neighborhood of the river warned the people that the flood was at hand, they all engaged busily in the work of completing their preparations. The harvests were all gathered from the fields, and the vast stores of fruit and corn which they yielded were piled in roofless granaries, built on every elevated spot of ground, where they would be safe from the approaching inundation. The rise of the water was very gradual and slow. Streams began to flow in all directions over the land. Ponds and lakes, growing every day more and more extended, spread mysteriously over the surface of the meadows; and all the time while this deluge of water was rising to submerge the land, the air continued dry, the sun was sultry, and the sky was without a cloud.

As the flood continued to rise, the proportion of land and water, and the conformation of the irregular and temporary shores which separated them, were changed continually, from day to day. The inhabitants assembled in their villages, which were built on rising grounds, some natural, others artificially formed. The waters rose more and more, until only these crowded islands appeared above its surface—when, at length, the valley presented to the view the spectacle of a vast expanse of water, calm as a summer's sea, brilliant with the reflected rays of a tropical sun, and canopied by a sky, which, displaying its spotless blue by day and its countless stars at night, was always cloudless and serene.

The inundation was at its height in October. After that period the waters gradually subsided, leaving a slimy and very fertilizing deposit all over the lands which they had covered. Though the inhabitants themselves, who had been accustomed to this overflow from infancy, felt no wonder or curiosity about its cause, the philosophers of the day, and travelers from other countries who visited Egypt, made many attempts to seek an explanation of the phenomenon. They had three theories on the subject, which Herodotus mentions and discusses.

The first explanation was, that the rising of the river was occasioned by the prevalence of northerly winds on the Mediterranean at that time of the year, which drove back the waters at the mouth of the river, and so caused the accumulation of the water in the upper parts of the valley. Herodotus thought that this was not a satisfactory explanation; for sometimes, as he said, these northerly winds did not blow, and yet the rising of the river took place none the less when the appointed season came. Besides, there were other rivers similarly situated in respect to the influence of prevailing winds at sea in driving in the waters at their mouths, which were, nevertheless, not subject to inundations like the Nile.

The second theory was, that the Nile took its rise, not, like other rivers, in inland lakes, or among inland mountains, but in some remote and unknown ocean on the other side of the continent, which ocean the advocates of this theory supposed might be subject to some great annual ebb and flow; and from this it might result that at stated periods an unusual tide of waters might be poured into the channel of the river. This, however, could not be true, for the waters of the inundation were fresh, not salt, which proved that they were not furnished by any ocean.

A third hypothesis was, that the rising of the water was occasioned by the melting of the snows in summer on the mountains from which the sources of the river came. Against this supposition Herodotus found more numerous and more satisfactory reasons even than he had advanced against the others. In the first place the river came from the south—a direction in which the heat increased in intensity with every league, as far as travelers had explored it; and beyond those limits, they supposed that the burning sun made the country uninhabitable. It was preposterous to suppose that there could be snow and ice there. Then, besides, the Nile had been ascended to a great distance, and reports from the natives had been brought down from regions still more remote, and no tidings had ever been brought of ice and snow. It was unreasonable, therefore, to suppose that the inundations could arise from such a cause.

These scientific theories, however, were discussed only among philosophers and learned men. The common people had a much more simple and satisfactory mode of disposing of the subject. They, in their imaginations, invested the beneficent river with a sort of life and personality, and when they saw its waters rising so gently but yet surely, to overflow their whole land, leaving it, as they withdrew again, endued with a new and exuberant fertility, they imagined it a living and acting intelligence, that in the exercise of some mysterious and inscrutable powers, the nature of which was to them unknown, and impelled by a kind and friendly regard for the country and its inhabitants, came annually, of its own accord, to spread over the land the blessings of fertility and abundance. The mysterious stream being viewed in this light, its wonderful powers awakened their veneration and awe, and its boundless beneficence their gratitude.

Pheron Defying the Nile.

Among the ancient Egyptian legends, there is one relating to a certain King Pheron which strikingly illustrates this feeling. It seems that during one of the inundations, while he was standing with his courtiers and watching the flow of the water, the commotion in the stream was much greater than usual on account of a strong wind which was blowing at that time, and which greatly increased the violence of the whirlpools, and the force and swell of the boiling eddies. There was given, in fact, to the appearance of the river an expression of anger, and Pheron, who was of a proud and haughty character, like most of the Egyptian kings, threw his javelin into one of the wildest of the whirlpools, as a token of his defiance of its rage. He was instantly struck blind!

The sequel of the story is curious, though it has no connection with the personality of the Nile. Pheron remained blind for ten years. At the end of that time it was announced to him, by some supernatural communication, that the period of his punishment had expired, and that his sight might be brought back to him by the employment of a certain designated means of restoration, which was the bathing of his eyes by a strictly virtuous woman. Pheron undertook compliance with the requisition, without any idea that the finding of a virtuous woman would be a difficult task. He first tried his own wife, but her bathing produced no effect. He then tried, one after another, various ladies of his court, and afterward others of different rank and station, selecting those who were most distinguished for the excellence of their characters. He was disappointed, however, in them all. The blindness continued unchanged. At last, however, he found the wife of a peasant, whose bathing produced the effect. The monarch's sight was suddenly restored. The king rewarded the peasant woman, whose virtuous character was established by this indisputable test, with the highest honors. The others he collected together, and then shut them up in one of his towns. When they were all thus safely imprisoned, he set the town on fire, and burned them all up together.

To return to the Nile. Certain columns were erected in different parts of the valley, on which cubits and the subdivisions of cubits were marked and numbered, for the purpose of ascertaining precisely the rise of the water. Such a column was called a Nilometer. There was one near Memphis, which was at the upper point of the Delta, and others further up the river. Such pillars continue to be used to mark the height of the inundations to the present day.

The object of thus accurately ascertaining the rise of the water was not mere curiosity, for there were certain important business operations which depended upon the results. The fertility and productiveness of the soil each year were determined almost wholly by the extent of the inundation; and as the ability of the people to pay tribute depended upon their crops, the Nilometer furnished the government with a criterion by which they regulated the annual assessments of the taxes. There were certain canals, too, made to convey the water to distant tracts of land, which were opened or kept closed according as the water rose to a higher or lower point. All these things were regulated by the indications of the Nilometer.

Egypt was famed in the days of Xerxes for those enormous structures and ruins of structures whose origin was then, as now, lost in a remote antiquity. Herodotus found the Pyramids standing in his day, and presenting the same spectacle of mysterious and solitary grandeur which they exhibited to Napoleon. He speculated on their origin and their history, just as the philosophers and travelers of our day do. In fact, he knew less and could learn less about them than is known now. It helps to impress our minds with an idea of the extreme antiquity of these and the other architectural wonders of Egypt, to compare them with things which are considered old in the Western world. The ancient and venerable colleges and halls of Oxford and Cambridge are, many of them, two or three hundred years old. There are remains of the old wall of the city of London which has been standing seven hundred years. This is considered a great antiquity. There are, however, Roman ruins in Britain, and in various parts of Europe, more ancient still. They have been standing eighteen hundred years! People look upon these with a species of wonder and awe that they have withstood the destructive influences of time so long. But as to the Pyramids, if we go back twenty-five hundred years, we find travelers visiting and describing them then —monuments as ancient, as venerable, as mysterious and unknown in their eyes, as they appear now in ours. We judge that a mountain is very distant when, after traveling many miles toward it, it seems still as distant as ever. Now, in tracing the history of the pyramids, the obelisks, the gigantic statues, and the vast columnar ruins of the Nile, we may go back twenty-five hundred years, without, apparently, making any progress whatever toward reaching their origin.

Such was Egypt. Isolated as it was from the rest of the world, and full of fertility and riches, it offered a marked and definite object to the ambition of a conqueror. In fact, on account of the peculiar interest which this long and narrow valley of verdure, with its wonderful structures, the strange and anomalous course of nature which prevails in it, and the extraordinary phases which human life, in consequence, exhibits there, has always excited among mankind, heroes and conquerors have generally considered it a peculiarly glorious field for their exploits. Cyrus, the founder of the Persian monarchy, contemplated the subjugation of it. He did not carry his designs into effect, but left them for Cambyses his son. Darius held the country as a dependency during his reign, though, near the close of his life, it revolted. This revolt took place while he was preparing for his grand expedition against Greece, and he was perplexed with the question which of the two undertakings, the subjugation of the Egyptians or the invasion of Greece, he should first engage in. In the midst of this uncertainty he suddenly died, leaving both the wars themselves and the perplexity of deciding between them as a part of the royal inheritance falling to his son.

Xerxes decided to prosecute the Egyptian campaign first, intending to postpone the conquest of Greece till he had brought the valley of the Nile once more under Persian sway. He deemed it dangerous to leave a province of his father's empire in a state of successful rebellion, while leading his armies off to new undertakings. Mardonius, who was the commander-in-chief of the army, and the great general on whom Xerxes mainly relied for the execution of his schemes, was very reluctant to consent to this plan. He was impatient for the conquest of Greece. There was little glory for him to acquire in merely suppressing a revolt, and reconquering what had been already once subdued. He was eager to enter upon a new field. Xerxes, however, overruled his wishes, and the armies commenced their march for Egypt. They passed the land of Judea on their way, where the captives who had returned from Babylon, and their successors, were rebuilding the cities and reoccupying the country. Xerxes confirmed them in the privileges which Cyrus and Darius had granted them, and aided them in their work. He then went on toward the Nile. The rebellion was easily put down. In less than a year from the time of leaving Susa, he had reconquered the whole land of Egypt, punished the leaders of the revolt, established his brother as viceroy of the country, and returned in safety to Susa.

All this took place in the second year of his reign.

3

Debate on the Proposed Invasion of Greece

B.C. 481

Counselors of Xerxes.—Age and character of Mardonius.—The avenues to renown.—Blood inherited and blood shed.—Character of Artabanus.—His advice to Xerxes.—The Ionian rebellion.—First invasion of Greece.—Xerxes convenes a public council.—His speech.—Xerxes recounts the aggressions of the Athenians.—Xerxes proposes to build a bridge over the Hellespont.—Excitement of Mardonius.—His speech.—Mardonius expresses his contempt of the Greeks.—Predictions of Mardonius.—Pause in the assembly.—Speech of Artabanus.—His apologies.—Artabanus opposes the war.—Repulse of Datis.—Artabanus warns Xerxes of the danger of the expedition.—Artabanus vindicates the character of the Greeks.—Xerxes's displeasure.—His angry reply to Artabanus.—Xerxes's anxiety.—He determines to abandon his project.—Xerxes sees a vision in the night.—The spirit appears a second time to Xerxes.—Xerxes relates his dreams to Artabanus.—Opinion of the latter.—Artabanus takes Xerxes's place.—The spirit appears a third time.—Artabanus is convinced.—The invasion decided upon.—Mardonius probably the ghost.

THE two great counselors on whose judgment Xerxes mainly relied, so far as he looked to any other judgment than his own in the formation of his plans, were Artabanus, the uncle by whose decision the throne had been awarded to him, and Mardonius, the commander-in-chief of his armies. Xerxes himself was quite a young man, of a proud and lofty, yet generous character, and full of self-confidence and hope. Mardonius was much older, but he was a soldier by profession, and was eager to distinguish himself in some great military campaign. It has always been unfortunate for the peace and happiness of mankind, under all monarchical and despotic governments, in every age of the world, that, through some depraved and unaccountable perversion of public sentiment, those who are not born to greatness have had no means of attaining to it except as heroes in war. Many men have, indeed, by their mental powers or their moral excellences, acquired an extended and lasting posthumous fame; but in respect to all immediate and exalted distinction and honor, it will be found, on reviewing the history of the human race, that there have generally been but two possible avenues to them: on the one hand, high birth, and on the other, the performance of great deeds of carnage and destruction. There must be, it seems, as the only valid claim to renown, either blood inherited or blood shed. The glory of the latter is second, indeed, to that of the former, but it is only second. He who has sacked a city stands very high in the estimation of his fellows. He yields precedence only to him whose grandfather sacked one.

This state of things is now, it is true, rapidly undergoing a change. The age of chivalry, of military murder and robbery, and of the glory of great deeds of carnage and blood, is passing away, and that of peace, of industry, and of achievements for promoting the comfort and happiness of mankind is coming. The men who are now advancing to the notice of the world are those who, through their commerce or their manufactures, feed and clothe their fellow-men by millions, or, by opening new channels or new means for international intercourse, civilize savages, and people deserts; while the glory of killing and destroying is less and less regarded, and more and more readily forgotten.

In the days of Xerxes, however, there was no road to honor but by war, and Mardonius found that his only hope of rising to distinction was by conducting a vast torrent of military devastation over some portion of the globe; and the fairer, the richer, the happier the scene which he was thus to inundate and overwhelm, the greater would be the glory. He was very much disposed, therefore, to urge on the invasion of Greece by every means in his power.

Artabanus, on the other hand, the uncle of Xerxes, was a man advanced in years, and of a calm and cautious disposition. He was better aware than younger men of the vicissitudes and hazards of war, and was much more inclined to restrain than to urge on the youthful ambition of his nephew. Xerxes had been able to present some show of reason for his campaign in Egypt, by calling the resistance which that country offered to his power a rebellion. There was, however, no such reason in the case of Greece. There had been two wars between Persia and the Athenians already, it is true. In the first, the Athenians had aided their countrymen in Asia Minor in a fruitless attempt to recover their independence. This the Persian government considered as aiding and abetting a rebellion. In the second, the Persians under Datis, one of Darius's generals, had undertaken a grand invasion of Greece, and, after landing in the neighborhood of Athens, were beaten, with immense slaughter, at the great battle of Marathon, near that city. The former of these wars is known in history as the Ionian rebellion; the latter as the first Persian invasion of Greece. They had both occurred during the reign of Darius, and the invasion under Datis had taken place not many years before the accession of Xerxes, so that a great number of the officers who had served in that campaign were still remaining in the court and army of Xerxes at Susa. These wars had, however, both been terminated, and Artabanus was very little inclined to have the contests renewed.

Xerxes, however, was bent upon making one more attempt to conquer Greece, and when the time arrived for commencing his preparations, he called a grand council of the generals, the nobles, and the potentates of the realm, to lay his plans before them. The historian who narrated these proceedings recorded the debate that ensued in the following manner.

Xerxes himself first addressed the assembly, to announce and explain his designs.

"The enterprise, my friends," said he, "in which I propose now to engage, and in which I am about to ask your co-operation, is no new scheme of my own devising. What I design to do is, on the other hand, only the carrying forward of the grand course of measures marked out by my predecessors, and pursued by them with steadiness and energy, so long as the power remained in their hands. That power has now descended to me, and with it has devolved the responsibility of finishing the work which they so successfully began.

"It is the manifest destiny of Persia to rule the world. From the time that Cyrus first commenced the work of conquest by subduing Media, to the present day, the extent of our empire has been continually widening, until now it covers all of Asia and Africa, with the exception of the remote and barbarous tribes, that, like the wild beasts which share their forests with them, are not worth the trouble of subduing. These vast conquests have been made by the courage, the energy, and the military power of Cyrus, Darius, and Cambyses, my renowned predecessors. They, on their part, have subdued Asia and Africa; Europe remains. It devolves on me to finish what they have begun. Had my father lived, he would, himself, have completed the work. He had already made great preparations for the undertaking; but he died, leaving the task to me, and it is plain that I can not hesitate to undertake it without a manifest dereliction of duty.

"You all remember the unprovoked and wanton aggressions which the Athenians committed against us in the time of the Ionian rebellion, taking part against us with rebels and enemies. They crossed the Ægean

Sea on that occasion, invaded our territories, and at last captured and burned the city of Sardis, the principal capital of our Western empire. I will never rest until I have had my revenge by burning Athens. Many of you, too, who are here present, remember the fate of the expedition under Datis. Those of you who were attached to that expedition will have no need that I should urge you to seek revenge for your own wrongs. I am sure that you will all second my undertaking with the utmost fidelity and zeal.

"My plan for gaining access to the Grecian territories is not, as before, to convey the troops by a fleet of galleys over the Ægean Sea, but to build a bridge across the Hellespont, and march the army to Greece by land. This course, which I am well convinced is practicable, will be more safe than the other, and the bridging of the Hellespont will be of itself a glorious deed. The Greeks will be utterly unable to resist the enormous force which we shall be able to pour upon them. We can not but conquer; and inasmuch as beyond the Greek territories there is, as I am informed, no other power at all able to cope with us, we shall easily extend our empire on every side to the sea, and thus the Persian dominion will cover the whole habitable world.

"I am sure that I can rely on your cordial and faithful co-operation in these plans, and that each one of you will bring me, from his own province or territories, as large a quota of men, and of supplies for the war, as is in his power. They who contribute thus most liberally I shall consider as entitled to the highest honors and rewards."

Such was, in substance, the address of Xerxes to his council. He concluded by saying that it was not his wish to act in the affair in an arbitrary or absolute manner, and he invited all present to express, with perfect freedom, any opinions or views which they entertained in respect to the enterprise.

While Xerxes had been speaking, the soul of Mardonius had been on fire with excitement and enthusiasm, and every word which the king had uttered only fanned the flame. He rose immediately when the king

THE HISTORY OF XERXES

gave permission to the counselors to speak, and earnestly seconded the monarch's proposals in the following words:

"For my part, sire, I can not refrain from expressing my high admiration of the lofty spirit and purpose on your part, which leads you to propose to us an enterprise so worthy of your illustrious station and exalted personal renown. Your position and power at the present time are higher than those ever attained by any human sovereign that has ever lived; and it is easy to foresee that there is a career of glory before you which no future monarch can ever surpass. You are about to complete the conquest of the world! That exploit can, of course, never be exceeded. We all admire the proud spirit on your part which will not submit tamely to the aggressions and insults which we have received from the Greeks. We have conquered the people of India, of Egypt, of Ethiopia, and of Assyria, and that, too, without having previously suffered any injury from them, but solely from a noble love of dominion; and shall we tamely stop in our career when we see nations opposed to us from whom we have received so many insults, and endured so many wrongs? Every consideration of honor and manliness forbids it.

"We have nothing to fear in respect to the success of the enterprise in which you invite us to engage. I know the Greeks, and I know that they can not stand against our arms. I have encountered them many times and in various ways. I met them in the provinces of Asia Minor, and you all know the result. I met them during the reign of Darius your father, in Macedon and Thrace—or, rather, sought to meet them; for, though I marched through the country, the enemy always avoided me. They could not be found. They have a great name, it is true; but, in fact, all their plans and arrangements are governed by imbecility and folly. They are not ever united among themselves. As they speak one common language, any ordinary prudence and sagacity would lead them to combine together, and make common cause against the nations that surround them. Instead of this, they are divided into a multitude of petty states and kingdoms, and all their resources and power are exhausted in fruitless contentions with each other. I am convinced that, once across the

Hellespont, we can march to Athens without finding any enemy to oppose our progress; or, if we should encounter any resisting force, it will be so small and insignificant as to be instantly overwhelmed."

In one point Mardonius was nearly right in his predictions, since it proved subsequently, as will hereafter be seen, that when the Persian army reached the pass of Thermopylae, which was the great avenue of entrance, on the north, into the territories of the Greeks, they found only three hundred men ready there to oppose their passage!

When Mardonius had concluded his speech, he sat down, and quite a solemn pause ensued. The nobles and chieftains generally were less ready than he to encounter the hazards and uncertainties of so distant a campaign. Xerxes would acquire, by the success of the enterprise, a great accession to his wealth and to his dominion, and Mardonius, too, might expect to reap very rich rewards; but what were they themselves to gain? They did not dare, however, to seem to oppose the wishes of the king, and, notwithstanding the invitation which he had given them to speak, they remained silent, not knowing, in fact, exactly what to say.

All this time Artabanus, the venerable uncle of Xerxes, sat silent like the rest, hesitating whether his years, his rank, and the relation which he sustained to the young monarch would justify his interposing, and make it prudent and safe for him to attempt to warn his nephew of the consequences which he would hazard by indulging his dangerous ambition. At length he determined to speak.

"I hope," said he, addressing the king, "that it will not displease you to have other views presented in addition to those which have already been expressed. It is better that all opinions should be heard; the just and the true will then appear the more just and true by comparison with others. It seems to me that the enterprise which you contemplate is full of danger, and should be well considered before it is undertaken. When Darius, your father, conceived of the plan of his invasion of the country of the Scythians beyond the Danube, I counseled him against the attempt. The benefits to be secured by such an undertaking seemed to me wholly insufficient to compensate for the expense, the difficulties, and the dangers of it. My counsels were, however, overruled. Your father proceeded on the enterprise. He crossed the Bosporus, traversed Thrace, and then crossed the Danube; but, after a long and weary contest with the hordes of savages which he found in those trackless wilds, he was forced to abandon the undertaking, and return, with the loss of half his army. The plan which you propose seems to me to be liable to the same dangers, and I fear very much that it will lead to the same results.

"The Greeks have the name of being a valiant and formidable foe. It may prove in the end that they are so. They certainly repulsed Datis and all his forces, vast as they were, and compelled them to retire with an enormous loss. Your invasion, I grant, will be more formidable than his. You will throw a bridge across the Hellespont, so as to take your troops round through the northern parts of Europe into Greece, and you will also, at the same time, have a powerful fleet in the Ægean Sea. But it must be remembered that the naval armaments of the Greeks in all those waters are very formidable. They may attack and destroy your fleet. Suppose that they should do so, and that then, proceeding to the northward in triumph, they should enter the Hellespont and destroy your bridge? Your retreat would be cut off, and, in case of a reverse of fortune, your army would be exposed to total ruin.

"Your father, in fact, very narrowly escaped precisely this fate. The Scythians came to destroy his bridge across the Danube while his forces were still beyond the river, and, had it not been for the very extraordinary fidelity and zeal of Histiaeus, who had been left to guard the post, they would have succeeded in doing it. It is frightful to think that the whole Persian army, with the sovereign of the empire at their head, were placed in a position where their being saved from overwhelming and total destruction depended solely on the fidelity and firmness of a single man! Should you place your forces and your own person in the same danger, can you safely calculate upon the same fortunate escape?

"Even the very vastness of your force may be the means of insuring and accelerating its destruction, since whatever rises to extraordinary elevation and greatness is always exposed to dangers correspondingly extraordinary and great. Thus tall trees and lofty towers seem always specially to invite the thunderbolts of Heaven.

"Mardonius charges the Greeks with a want of sagacity, efficiency, and valor, and speaks contemptuously of them, as soldiers, in every respect. I do not think that such imputations are just to the people against whom they are directed, or honorable to him who makes them. To disparage the absent, especially an absent enemy, is not magnanimous or wise; and I very much fear that it will be found in the end that the conduct of the Greeks will evince very different military qualities from those which Mardonius has assigned them. They are represented by common fame as sagacious, hardy, efficient, and brave, and it may prove that these representations are true.

"My counsel therefore is, that you dismiss this assembly, and take further time to consider this subject before coming to a final decision. Perhaps, on more mature reflection, you will conclude to abandon the project altogether. If you should not conclude to abandon it, but should decide, on the other hand, that it must be prosecuted, let me entreat you not to go yourself in company with the expedition. Let Mardonius take the charge and the responsibility. If he does so, I predict that he will leave the dead bodies of the soldiers that you intrust to him, to be devoured by dogs on the plains of Athens or Lacedaemon."

Xerxes was exceedingly displeased at hearing such a speech as this from his uncle, and he made a very angry reply. He accused Artabanus of meanness of spirit, and of a cowardice disgraceful to his rank and station, in thus advocating a tame submission to the arrogant pretensions of the Greeks. Were it not, he said, for the respect which he felt for Artabanus, as his father's brother, he would punish him severely for his presumption in thus basely opposing his sovereign's plans. "As it is," continued he, "I will carry my plans into effect, but you shall not have the honor of accompanying me. You shall remain at Susa with the women and children of the palace, and spend your time in the effeminate and ignoble pleasures suited to a spirit so mean. As for myself, I must and will carry my designs into execution. I could not, in fact, long avoid a contest with the Greeks, even if I were to adopt the cowardly and degrading policy which you recommend; for I am confident that they will very soon invade my dominions, if I do not anticipate them by invading theirs."

So saying, Xerxes dismissed the assembly.

His mind, however, was not at ease. Though he had so indignantly rejected the counsel which Artabanus had offered him, yet the impressive words in which it had been uttered, and the arguments with which it had been enforced, weighed upon his spirit, and oppressed and dejected him. The longer he considered the subject, the more serious his doubts and fears became, until at length, as the night approached, he became convinced that Artabanus was right, and that he himself was wrong. His mind found no rest until he came to the determination to abandon the project after all. He resolved to make this change in his resolution known to Artabanus and his nobles in the morning, and to countermand the orders which he had given for the assembling of the troops. Having by this decision restored something like repose to his agitated mind, he laid himself down upon his couch and went to sleep.

In the night he saw a vision. It seemed to him that a resplendent and beautiful form appeared before him, and after regarding him a moment with an earnest look, addressed him as follows:

"And do you really intend to abandon your deliberate design of leading an array into Greece, after having formally announced it to the realm and issued your orders? Such fickleness is absurd, and will greatly dishonor you. Resume your plan, and go on boldly and perseveringly to the execution of it."

So saying, the vision disappeared.

When Xerxes awoke in the morning, and the remembrance of the events of the preceding day returned, mingling itself with the new impressions which had been made by the dream, he was again agitated and perplexed. As, however, the various influences which pressed upon him settled to their final equilibrium, the fears produced by Artabanus's substantial arguments and warnings on the preceding day proved to be of greater weight than the empty appeal to his pride which had been made by the phantom of the night. He resolved to persist in the abandonment of his scheme. He called his council, accordingly, together again, and told them that, on more mature reflection, he had become convinced that his uncle was right and that he himself had been wrong. The project, therefore, was for the present suspended, and the orders for the assembling of the forces were revoked. The announcement was received by the members of the council with the most tumultuous joy.

That night Xerxes had another dream. The same spirit appeared to him again, his countenance, however, bearing now, instead of the friendly look of the preceding night, a new and stern expression of displeasure. Pointing menacingly at the frightened monarch with his finger, he exclaimed, "You have rejected my advice; you have abandoned your plan; and now I declare to you that, unless you immediately resume your enterprise and carry it forward to the end, short as has been the time since you were raised to your present elevation, a still shorter period shall elapse before your downfall and destruction."

The spirit then disappeared as suddenly as it came, leaving Xerxes to awake in an agony of terror.

As soon as it was day, Xerxes sent for Artabanus, and related to him his dreams. "I was willing," said he, "after hearing what you said, and maturely considering the subject, to give up my plan; but these dreams, I can not but think, are intimations from Heaven that I ought to proceed."

Artabanus attempted to combat this idea by representing to Xerxes that dreams were not to be regarded as indications of the will of Heaven, but only as a vague and disordered reproduction of the waking thoughts, while the regular action of the reason and the judgment by which they were ordinarily controlled was suspended or disturbed by the influence of slumber. Xerxes maintained, on the other hand, that, though this view of the case might explain his first vision, the solemn repetition of the warning proved that it was supernatural and divine. He proposed that, to put the reality of the apparition still further to the test, Artabanus should take his place on the royal couch the next night, to see if the specter would not appear to him. "You shall clothe yourself," said he, "in my robes, put the crown upon your head, and take your seat upon the throne. After that, you shall retire to my apartment, lie down upon the couch, and go to sleep. If the vision is supernatural, it will undoubtedly appear to you. If it does not so appear, I will admit that it was nothing but a dream."

Artabanus made some objection, at first, to the details of the arrangement which Xerxes proposed, as he did not see, he said, of what advantage it could be for him to assume the guise and habiliments of the king. If the vision was divine, it could not be deceived by such artifices as those. Xerxes, however, insisted on his proposition, and Artabanus yielded. He assumed for an hour the dress and the station of the king, and then retired to the king's apartment, and laid himself down upon the couch under the royal pavilion. As he had no faith in the reality of the vision, his mind was quiet and composed, and he soon fell asleep.

At midnight, Xerxes, who was lying in an adjoining apartment, was suddenly aroused by a loud and piercing cry from the room where Artabanus was sleeping, and in a moment afterward Artabanus himself rushed in, perfectly wild with terror. He had seen the vision. It had appeared before him with a countenance and gestures expressive of great displeasure, and after loading him with reproaches for having attempted to keep Xerxes back from his proposed expedition into Greece, it attempted to bore out his eyes with a red-hot iron with which it was armed. Artabanus had barely succeeded in escaping by leaping from his couch and rushing precipitately out of the room.

Artabanus said that he was now convinced and satisfied. It was plainly the divine will that Xerxes should undertake his projected invasion, and he would himself, thenceforth, aid the enterprise by every means in his power. The council was, accordingly, once more convened. The story of the three apparitions was related to them, and the final decision announced that the armies were to be assembled for the march without any further delay.

***

It is proper here to repeat, once for all in this volume, a remark which has elsewhere often been made in the various works of this series, that in studying ancient history at the present day, it is less important now to know, in regard to transactions so remote, what the facts actually were which really occurred, than it is to know the story respecting them, which, for the last two thousand years, has been in circulation among mankind. It is now, for example, of very little consequence whether there ever was or never was such a personage as Hercules, but it is essential that every educated man should know the story which ancient writers tell in relating his doings. In this view of the case, our object, in this volume, is simply to give the history of Xerxes just as it stands, without stopping to separate the false from the true. In relating the occurrences, therefore, which have been described in this chapter, we simply give the alleged facts to our readers precisely as the ancient historians give them to us, leaving each reader to decide for himself how far he will believe the narrative. In respect to this particular story, we will add, that some people think that Mardonius was really the ghost by whose appearance Artabanus and Xerxes were so dreadfully frightened.

4

Preparations for the Invasion of Greece

B.C. 481

Orders to the provinces.—Mode of raising money.—Modern mode of securing supplies of arms and money.—Xerxes's preparations.—Four years allotted to them.—Arms.—Provisions.—Building of ships.—Persian possessions on the north of the Ægean Sea.—Promontory of Mount Athos.—Dangerous navigation.—Plan of Xerxes for the march of his expedition.—Former shipwreck of Mardonius.—Terrible gale.—Destruction of Mardonius's fleet at Mount Athos.—Plan of a canal.—The Greeks do not interfere.—Plans of the engineers.—Prosecution of the work.—The Strymon bridged.—Granaries and store-houses.—Xerxes leaves Susa, and begins his march.—The Meander.—Celaenae.—Pythius.—The wealth of Pythius.—His interview with Xerxes.—The amount of Pythius's wealth. —His offer to Xerxes.—Gratification of Xerxes.—His reply to Pythius's offer.—Real character of Pythius.—The entertainment of silver and gold. —Xerxes's gratitude put to the test.—He murders Pythius's son.—Various objects of interest observed by the army.—The plane-tree.—Artificial honey.—Salt lake.—Gold and silver mines.—Xerxes summons the Greeks to surrender.—They indignantly refuse.

AS soon as the invasion of Greece was finally decided upon, the orders were transmitted to all the provinces of the empire, requiring the various authorities and powers to make the necessary preparations. There were men to be levied, arms to be manufactured, ships to be built, and stores of food to be provided. The expenditures, too, of so vast an armament as Xerxes was intending to organize, would require a large supply of money. For all these things Xerxes relied on the revenues and the contributions of the provinces, and orders, very full and very imperative, were transmitted, accordingly, to all the governors and satraps of Asia, and especially to those who ruled over the countries which lay near the western confines of the empire, and consequently near the Greek frontiers.

In modern times it is the practice of powerful nations to accumulate arms and munitions of war on storage in arsenals and naval depôts, so that the necessary supplies for very extended operations, whether of attack or defense, can be procured in a very short period of time. In respect to funds, too, modern nations have a great advantage over those of former days, in case of any sudden emergency arising to call for great and unusual expenditures. In consequence of the vast accumulation of capital in the hands of private individuals, and the confidence which is felt in the mercantile honor and good faith of most established governments at the present day, these governments can procure indefinite supplies of gold and silver at any time, by promising to pay an annual interest in lieu of the principal borrowed. It is true that, in these cases, a stipulation is made, by which the government may, at a certain specified period, pay back the principal, and so extinguish the annuity; but in respect to a vast portion of the amount so borrowed, it is not expected that this repayment will ever be made. The creditors, in fact, do not desire that it should be, as owners of property always prefer a safe annual income from it to the custody of the principal; and thus governments in good credit have sometimes induced their creditors to abate the rate of interest which they were receiving, by threatening otherwise to pay the debt in full.

These inventions, however, by which a government in one generation may enjoy the pleasure and reap the glory of waging war, and throw the burden of the expense on another, were not known in ancient times. Xerxes did not understand the art of funding a national debt, and there would, besides, have probably been very little confidence in Persian stocks, if any had been issued. He had to raise all his funds by actual taxation, and to have his arms, and his ships and chariots of war, manufactured express. The food, too, to sustain the immense army which he was to raise, was all to be produced, and store-houses were to be built for the accumulation and custody of it. All this, as might naturally be expected, would require time; and the vastness of the scale on which these immense preparations were made is evinced by the fact that four years were the time allotted for completing them. This period includes, however, a considerable time before the great debate on the subject described in the last chapter.

The chief scene of activity, during all this time, was the tract of country in the western part of Asia Minor, and along the shores of the Ægean Sea. Taxes and contributions were raised from all parts of the empire, but the actual material of war was furnished mainly from those provinces which were nearest to the future scene of it. Each district provided such things as it naturally and most easily produced. One contributed horses, another arms and ammunition, another ships, and another provisions. The ships which were built were of various forms and modes of construction, according to the purposes which they were respectively intended to serve. Some were strictly ships of war, intended for actual combat; others were transports, their destination being simply the conveyance of troops or of military stores. There were also a large number of vessels, which were built on a peculiar model, prescribed by the engineers, being very long and straight-sided, and smooth and flat upon their decks. These were intended for the bridge across the Hellespont. They were made long, so that, when placed side by side across the stream, a greater breadth might be given to the platform of the bridge. All these things were very deliberately and carefully planned.

Although it was generally on the Asiatic side of the Ægean Sea that these vast works of preparation were going on, and the crossing of the Hellespont was to be the first great movement of the Persian army, the reader must not suppose that, even at this time, the European shores were wholly in the hands of the Greeks. The Persians had, long before, conquered Thrace and a part of Macedon; and thus the northern shores of the Ægean Sea, and many of the islands, were already in Xerxes's hands. The Greek dominions lay further south, and Xerxes did not anticipate any opposition from the enemy, until his army, after crossing the strait, should have advanced to the neighborhood of Athens. In fact, all the northern country through which his route would lie was already in his hands, and in passing through it he anticipated no difficulties except such as should arise from the elements themselves, and the physical obstacles of the way. The Hellespont itself was, of course, one principal point of danger. The difficulty here was to be surmounted by the bridge of boats. There was, however, another point, which was, in some respects, still more formidable: it was the promontory of Mount Athos.

By looking at the map of Greece, placed at the commencement of the next chapter, the reader will see that there are two or three singular promontories jutting out from the main land in the northwestern part of the Ægean Sea. The most northerly and the largest of these was formed by an immense mountainous mass rising out of the water, and connected by a narrow isthmus with the main land. The highest summit of this rocky pile was called Mount Athos in ancient times, and is so marked upon the map. In modern days it is called Monte Santo, or Holy Mountain, being covered with monasteries, and convents, and other ecclesiastical establishments built in the Middle Ages.

Mount Athos is very celebrated in ancient history. It extended along the promontory for many miles, and terminated abruptly in lofty cliffs and precipices toward the sea, where it was so high that its shadow, as was said, was thrown, at sunset, across the water to the island of Lemnos, a distance of twenty leagues. It was a frightful specter in the eyes of the ancient navigators, when, as they came coasting along from the north in their frail galleys, on their voyages to Greece and Italy, they saw it frowning defiance to them as they came, with threatening clouds hanging upon its summit, and the surges and surf of the Ægean perpetually thundering upon its base below. To make this stormy promontory the more terrible, it was believed to be the haunt of innumerable uncouth and misshapen monsters of the sea, that lived by devouring the hapless seamen who were thrown upon the rocks from their wrecked vessels by the merciless tumult of the waves.

The plan which Xerxes had formed for the advance of his expedition was, that the army which was to cross the Hellespont by the bridge should advance thence through Macedonia and Thessaly, by land, attended by a squadron of ships, transports, and galleys, which was to accompany the expedition along the coast by sea. The men could be marched more conveniently to their place of destination by land. The stores, on the other hand, the arms, the supplies, and the baggage of every description, could be transported more easily by sea. Mardonius was somewhat solicitous in respect to the safety of the great squadron which would be required for this latter service, in doubling the promontory of Mount Athos.

In fact, he had special and personal reason for his solicitude, for he had himself, some years before, met with a terrible disaster at this very spot. It was during the reign of Darius that this disaster occurred. On one of the expeditions which Darius had intrusted to his charge, he was conducting a very large fleet along the coast, when a sudden storm arose just as he was approaching this terrible promontory.

He was on the northern side of the promontory when the storm came on, and as the wind was from the north, it blew directly upon the shore. For the fleet to make its escape from the impending danger, it seemed necessary, therefore, to turn the course of the ships back against the wind; but this, on account of the sudden and terrific violence of the gale, it was impossible to do. The sails, when they attempted to use them, were blown away by the howling gusts, and the oars were broken to pieces by the tremendous dashing of the sea. It soon appeared that the only hope of escape for the squadron was to press on in the desperate attempt to double the promontory, and thus gain, if possible, the sheltered water under its lee. The galleys, accordingly, went on, the pilots and the seamen exerting their utmost to keep them away from the shore.

All their efforts, however, to do this, were vain. The merciless gales drove the vessels, one after another, upon the rocks, and dashed them to pieces, while the raging sea wrenched the wretched mariners from the wrecks to which they attempted to cling, and tossed them out into the boiling whirlpools around, to the monsters that were ready there to devour them, as if she were herself some ferocious monster, feeding her offspring with their proper prey. A few, it is true, of the hapless wretches succeeded in extricating themselves from the surf, by crawling up upon the rocks, through the tangled sea-weed, until they were above the reach of the surges; but when they had done so, they found themselves hopelessly imprisoned between the impending precipices which frowned above them and the frantic billows which were raging and roaring below. They gained, of course, by their apparent escape, only a brief prolongation of suffering, for they all soon miserably perished from exhaustion, exposure, and cold.

Mardonius had no desire to encounter this danger again. Now the promontory of Mount Athos, though high and rocky itself, was connected with the main land by an isthmus level and low, and not very broad. Xerxes determined on cutting a canal through this isthmus, so as to take his fleet of galleys across the neck, and thus avoid the stormy navigation of the outward passage. Such a canal would be of service not merely for the passage of the great fleet, but for the constant communication which it would be necessary for Xerxes to maintain with his own dominions during the whole period of the invasion.

It might have been expected that the Greeks would have interfered to prevent the execution of such a work as this; but it seems that they did not, and yet there was a considerable Greek population in that vicinity.

The promontory of Athos itself was quite extensive, being about thirty miles long and four or five wide, and it had several towns upon it. The canal which Xerxes was to cut across the neck of this peninsula was to be wide enough for two triremes to pass each other. Triremes were galleys propelled by three banks of oars, and were vessels of the largest class ordinarily employed; and as the oars by which they were impelled required almost as great a breadth of water as the vessels themselves, the canal was, consequently, to be very wide.

The engineers, accordingly, laid out the ground, and, marking the boundaries by stakes and lines, as guides to the workmen, the excavation was commenced. Immense numbers of men were set at work, arranged regularly in gangs, according to the various nations which furnished them. As the excavation gradually proceeded, and the trench began to grow deep, they placed ladders against the sides, and stationed a series of men upon them; then the earth dug from the bottom was hauled up from one to another, in a sort of basket or hod, until it reached the top, where it was taken by other men and conveyed away.

The work was very much interrupted and impeded, in many parts of the line, by the continual caving in of the banks, on account of the workmen attempting to dig perpendicularly down. In one section—the one which had been assigned to the Phoenicians—this difficulty did not occur; for the Phoenicians, more considerate than the rest, had taken the precaution to make the breadth of their part of the trench twice as great at the top as it was below. By this means the banks on each side were formed to a gradual slope, and consequently stood firm. The canal was at length completed, and the water was let in.

North of the promontory of Mount Athos the reader will find upon the map the River Strymon, flowing south, not far from the boundary between Macedon and Thrace, into the Ægean Sea. The army of Xerxes, in its march from the Hellespont, would, of course, have to cross this river; and Xerxes having, by cutting the canal across the isthmus of Mount Athos, removed an obstacle in the way of his fleet, resolved next to facilitate the progress of his army by bridging the Strymon.

The king also ordered a great number of granaries and store-houses to be built at various points along the route which it was intended that his army should pursue. Some of these were on the coasts of Macedonia and Thrace, and some on the banks of the Strymon. To these magazines the corn raised in Asia for the use of the expedition was conveyed, from time to time, in transport ships, as fast as it was ready, and, being safely deposited, was protected by a guard. No very extraordinary means of defense seems to have been thought necessary at these points, for, although the scene of all these preliminary arrangements was on the European side of the line, and in what was called Greek territory, still this part of the country had been long under Persian dominion. The independent states and cities of Greece were all further south, and the people who inhabited them did not seem disposed to interrupt these preparations. Perhaps they were not aware to what object and end all these formidable movements on their northern frontier were tending.

Xerxes, during all this time, had remained in Persia. The period at length arrived when, his preparations on the frontiers being far advanced toward completion, he concluded to move forward at the head of his forces to Sardis. Sardis was the great capital of the western part of his dominions, and was situated not far from the frontier. He accordingly assembled his forces, and, taking leave of his capital of Susa with much parade and many ceremonies, he advanced toward Asia Minor. Entering and traversing Asia Minor, he crossed the Halys, which had been, in former times, the western boundary of the empire, though its limits had now been extended very far beyond. Having crossed the Halys, the immense procession advanced into Phrygia.

A very romantic tale is told of an interview between Xerxes and a certain nobleman named Pythius, who resided in one of the Phrygian towns. The circumstances were these: After crossing the Halys, which river flows north into the Euxine Sea, the army went on to the westward through nearly the whole extent of Phrygia, until at length they came to the sources of the streams which flowed west into the Ægean Sea. One of the most remarkable of these rivers was the Meander. There was a town built exactly at the source of the Meander—so exactly, in fact, that the fountain from which the stream took its rise was situated in the public square of the town, walled in and ornamented like an artificial fountain in a modern city. The name of this town was Celaenae.

When the army reached Celaenae and encamped there, Pythius made a great entertainment for the officers, which, as the number was very large, was of course attended with an enormous expense. Not satisfied with this, Pythius sent word to the king that if he was, in any respect, in want of funds for his approaching campaign, he, Pythius, would take great pleasure in supplying him.

Xerxes was surprised at such proofs of wealth and munificence from a man in comparatively a private station. He inquired of his attendants who Pythius was. They replied that, next to Xerxes himself, he was the richest man in the world. They said, moreover, that he was as generous as he was rich. He had made Darius a present of a beautiful model of a fruit-tree and of a vine, of solid gold. He was by birth, they added, a Lydian.

Lydia was west of Phrygia, and was famous for its wealth. The River Pactolus, which was so celebrated for its golden sands, flowed through the country, and as the princes and nobles contrived to monopolize the treasures which were found, both in the river itself and in the mountains from which it flowed, some of them became immensely wealthy.

Xerxes was astonished at the accounts which he heard of Pythius's fortune. He sent for him, and asked him what was the amount of his treasures. This was rather an ominous question; for, under such despotic governments as those of the Persian kings, the only real safeguard of wealth was, often, the concealment of it. Inquiry on the part of a government, in respect to treasures accumulated by a subject, was, often, only a preliminary to the seizure and confiscation of them.

Pythius, however, in reply to the king's question, said that he had no hesitation in giving his majesty full information in respect to his fortune. He had been making, he said, a careful calculation of the amount of it, with a view of determining how much he could offer to contribute in aid of the Persian campaign. He found, he said, that he had two thousand talents of silver, and four millions, wanting seven thousand, of staters of gold.

The stater was a Persian coin. Even if we knew, at the present day, its exact value, we could not determine the precise amount denoted by the sum which Pythius named, the value of money being subject to such vast fluctuations in different ages of the world. Scholars who have taken an interest in inquiring into such points as these, have come to the conclusion that the amount of gold and silver coin which Pythius thus reported to Xerxes was equal to about thirty millions of dollars.

Pythius added, after stating the amount of the gold and silver which he had at command, that it was all at the service of the king for the purpose of carrying on the war. He had, he said, besides his money, slaves and farms enough for his own maintenance.

Xerxes was extremely gratified at this generosity, and at the proof which it afforded of the interest which Pythius felt in the cause of the king. "You are the only man," said he, "who has offered hospitality to me or to my army since I set out upon this march, and, in addition to your hospitality, you tender me your whole fortune. I will not, however, deprive you of your treasure. I will, on the contrary, order my treasurer to pay to you the seven thousand staters necessary to make your four millions complete. I offer you also my friendship, and will do any thing in my power, now and hereafter, to serve you. Continue to live in the enjoyment of your fortune. If you always act under the influence of the noble and generous impulses which govern you now, you will never cease to be prosperous and happy."

If we could end the account of Pythius and Xerxes here, what generous and noble-minded men we might suppose them to be! But alas! how large a portion of the apparent generosity and nobleness which shows itself among potentates and kings, turns into selfishness and hypocrisy when closely examined. Pythius was one of the most merciless tyrants that ever lived. He held all the people that lived upon his vast estates in a condition of abject slavery, compelling them to toil continually in his mines, in destitution and wretchedness, in order to add more and more to his treasures. The people came to his wife with their bitter complaints. She pitied them, but could not relieve them. One day, it is said that, in order to show her husband the vanity and folly of living only to amass silver and gold, and to convince him how little real power such treasures have to satisfy the wants of the human soul, she made him a great entertainment, in which there was a boundless profusion of wealth in the way of vessels and furniture of silver and gold, but scarcely any food. There was every thing to satisfy the eye with the sight of magnificence, but nothing to satisfy hunger. The noble guest sat starving in the midst of a scene of unexampled riches and splendor, because it was not possible to eat silver and gold.

And as for Xerxes's professions of gratitude and friendship for Pythius, they were put to the test, a short time after the transactions which we have above described, in a remarkable manner. Pythius had five sons. They were all in Xerxes's army. By their departure on the distant and dangerous expedition on which Xerxes was to lead them, their father would be left alone. Pythius, under these circumstances, resolved to venture so far on the sincerity of his sovereign's professions of regard as to request permission to retain one of his sons at home with his father, on condition of freely giving up the rest.

Xerxes, on hearing this proposal, was greatly enraged. "How dare you," said he, "come to me with such a demand? You and all that pertain to you are my slaves, and are bound to do my bidding without a murmur. You deserve the severest punishment for such an insolent request. In consideration, however, of your past good behavior, I will not inflict upon you what you deserve. I will only kill one of your sons —the one that you seem to cling to so fondly. I will spare the rest." So saying, the enraged king ordered the son whom Pythius had endeavored to retain to be slain before his eyes, and then directed that the dead body should be split in two, and the two halves thrown, the one on the right side of the road and the other on the left, that his army, as he said, might "march between them."

On leaving Phrygia, the army moved on toward the west. Their immediate destination as has already been said, was Sardis, where they were to remain until the ensuing spring. The historian mentions a number of objects of interest which attracted the attention of Xerxes and his officers on this march, which mark the geographical peculiarities of the country, or illustrate, in some degree, the ideas and manners of the times.

There was one town, for example, situated, not like Celaenae, where a river had its origin, but where one disappeared. The stream was a branch of the Meander. It came down from the mountains like any other mountain torrent, and then, at the town in question, it plunged suddenly down into a gulf or chasm and disappeared. It rose again at a considerable distance below, and thence flowed on, without any further evasions, to the Meander.

On the confines between Phrygia and Lydia the army came to a place where the road divided. One branch turned toward the north, and led to Lydia; the other inclined to the south, and conducted to Caria. Here, too, on the frontier, was a monument which had been erected by Croesus, the great king of Lydia, who lived in Cyrus's day, to mark the eastern boundaries of his kingdom. The Persians were, of course, much interested in looking upon this ancient landmark, which designated not only the eastern limit of Croesus's empire, but also what was, in ancient times, the western limit of their own.

There was a certain species of tree which grew in these countries called the plane-tree. Xerxes found one of these trees so large and beautiful that it attracted his special admiration. He took possession of it in his own name, and adorned it with golden chains, and set a guard over it. This idolization of a tree was a striking instance of the childish caprice and folly by which the actions of the ancient despots were so often governed.

As the army advanced, they came to other places of interest and objects of curiosity and wonder. There was a district where the people made a sort of artificial honey from grain, and a lake from which the inhabitants procured salt by evaporation, and mines, too, of silver and of gold. These objects interested and amused the minds of the Persians as they moved along, without, however, at all retarding or interrupting their progress. In due time they reached the great city of Sardis in safety, and here Xerxes established his head-quarters, and awaited the coming of spring.

In the mean time, however, he sent heralds into Greece to summon the country to surrender to him. This is a common formality when an army is about to attack either a town, a castle, or a kingdom. Xerxes's heralds crossed the Ægean Sea, and made their demands, in Xerxes's name, upon the Greek authorities. As might have been expected, the embassage was fruitless; and the heralds returned, bringing with them, from the Greeks, not acts or proffers of submission, but stern expressions of hostility and defiance. Nothing, of course, now remained, but that both parties should prepare for the impending crisis.

5

Crossing the Hellsepont

B.C. 480

Winter in Asia Minor.—Destruction of the bridge.—Indignation of Xerxes.—His ridiculous punishment of the sea.—Xerxes orders a new bridge to be made.—Its construction.—Mode of securing the boats.—The bridge finished.—Eclipse of the sun.—March from Sardis.—Order of march.—Car of Jupiter.—Chariot of Xerxes.—Camp followers.—Arrival at the plain of Troy.—The grand sacrifice.—Dejection of the army.—Mode of enlistment.—Condition of the soldiers.—Privations and hardships.—Storm on Mount Ida.—Abydos.—Parade of the troops.—Xerxes weeps.—The reason of it.—Comments of writers.—Remarks of Artabanus.—Conversation with Artabanus.—He renews his warnings.—Anxiety of Artabanus.—Xerxes is not convinced.—Advice of Artabanus in respect to employing the Ionians.—Xerxes's opinion of the Ionians.—Artabanus is permitted to return.—Sham sea fight.—Xerxes's address.—Crossing the bridge.—Preliminary ceremonies.—The order of march.—Movement of the fleet.—Time occupied in the passage.—Scene of confusion.

ALTHOUGH the ancient Asia Minor was in the same latitude as New York, there was yet very little winter there. Snows fell, indeed, upon the summits of the mountains, and ice formed occasionally upon quiet streams, and yet, in general, the imaginations of the inhabitants, in forming mental images of frost and snow, sought them not in their own winters, but in the cold and icy regions of the north, of which, however, scarcely any thing was known to them except what was disclosed by wild and exaggerated rumors and legends.

Map of Greece.

There was, however, a period of blustering winds and chilly rains which was called winter, and Xerxes was compelled to wait, before commencing his invasion, until the inclement season had passed. As it was, he did not wholly escape the disastrous effects of the wintery gales. A violent storm arose while he was at Sardis, and broke up the bridge which he had built across the Hellespont. When the tidings of this disaster were brought to Xerxes at his winter quarters, he was very much enraged. He was angry both with the sea for having destroyed the structure, and with the architects who had built it for not having made it strong enough to stand against its fury. He determined to punish both the waves and the workmen. He ordered the sea to be scourged with a monstrous whip, and directed that heavy chains should be thrown into it, as symbols of his defiance of its power, and of his determination to subject it to his control. The men who administered this senseless discipline cried out to the sea, as they did it, in the following words, which Xerxes had dictated to them: "Miserable monster! this is the punishment which Xerxes your master inflicts upon you, on account of the unprovoked and wanton injury you have done him. Be assured that he will pass over you, whether you will or no. He hates and defies you, object as you are, through your insatiable cruelty, and the nauseous bitterness of your waters, of the common abomination of mankind."

As for the men who had built the bridge, which had been found thus inadequate to withstand the force of a wintery tempest, he ordered every one of them to be beheaded.

The vengeance of the king being thus satisfied, a new set of engineers and workmen were designated and ordered to build another bridge. Knowing, as, of course, they now did, that their lives depended upon the stability of their structure, they omitted no possible precaution which could tend to secure it. They selected the strongest ships, and arranged them in positions which would best enable them to withstand the pressure of the current. Each vessel was secured in its place by strong anchors, placed scientifically in such a manner as to resist, to the best advantage, the force of the strain to which they would be exposed. There were two ranges of these vessels, extending from shore to shore, containing over three hundred in each. In each range one or two vessels were omitted, on the Asiatic side, to allow boats and galleys to pass through, in order to keep the communication open. These omissions did not interfere with the use of the bridge, as the superstructure and the roadway above was continued over them.

The vessels which were to serve for the foundation of the bridge being thus arranged and secured in their places, two immense cables were made and stretched from shore to shore, each being fastened, at the ends, securely to the banks, and resting in the middle on the decks of the vessels. For the fastenings of these cables on the shore there were immense piles driven into the ground, and huge rings attached to the piles. The cables, as they passed along the decks of the vessels over the water, were secured to them all by strong cordage, so that each vessel was firmly and indissolubly bound to all the rest.

Over these cables a platform was made of trunks of trees, with branches placed upon them to fill the interstices and level the surface. The whole was then covered with a thick stratum of earth, which made a firm and substantial road like that of a public highway. A high and close fence was also erected on each side, so as to shut off the view of the water, which might otherwise alarm the horses and the beasts of burden that were to cross with the army.

When the news was brought to Xerxes at Sardis that the bridge was completed, and that all things were ready for the passage, he made arrangements for commencing his march. A circumstance, however, here occurred that at first alarmed him. It was no less a phenomenon than an eclipse of the sun. Eclipses were considered in those days as extraordinary and supernatural omens, and Xerxes was naturally anxious to know what this sudden darkness was meant to portend. He directed the magi to consider the subject, and to give him their opinion. Their answer was, that, as the sun was the guardian divinity of the Greeks, and the moon that of the Persians, the meaning of the sudden withdrawal of the light of day doubtless was, that Heaven was about to withhold its protection from the Greeks in the approaching struggle. Xerxes was satisfied with this explanation, and the preparations for the march went on.

The movement of the grand procession from the city of Sardis was inconceivably splendid. First came the long trains of baggage, on mules, and camels, and horses, and other beasts of burden, attended by the drivers, and the men who had the baggage in charge. Next came an immense body of troops of all nations, marching irregularly, but under the command of the proper officers. Then, after a considerable interval, came a body of a thousand horse, splendidly caparisoned, and followed by a thousand spearmen, who marched trailing their spears upon the ground, in token of respect and submission to the king who was coming behind them.

Next to these troops, and immediately in advance of the king, were certain religious and sacred objects and personages, on which the people who gazed upon this gorgeous spectacle looked with the utmost awe and veneration. There were, first, ten sacred horses, splendidly caparisoned, each led by his groom, who was clothed in appropriate robes, as a sort of priest officiating in the service of a god. Behind these came the sacred car of Jupiter. This car was very large, and elaborately worked, and was profusely ornamented with gold. It was drawn by eight white horses. No human being was allowed to set his foot upon any part of it, and, consequently, the reins of the horses were carried back, under the car, to the charioteer, who walked behind. Xerxes's own chariot came next, drawn by very splendid horses, selected especially for their size and beauty. His charioteer, a young Persian noble, sat by his side.

Then came great bodies of troops. There was one corps of two thousand men, the life-guards of the king, who were armed in a very splendid and costly manner, to designate their high rank in the army, and the exalted nature of their duty as personal attendants on the sovereign. One thousand of these life-guards were foot soldiers, and the other thousand horsemen. After the life-guards came a body of ten thousand infantry, and after them ten thousand cavalry. This completed what was strictly the Persian part of the army. There was an interval of about a quarter of a mile in the rear of these bodies of troops, and then came a vast and countless multitude of servants, attendants, adventurers, and camp followers of every description—a confused, promiscuous, disorderly, and noisy throng.

The immediate destination of this vast horde was Abydos; for it was between Sestos, on the European shore, and Abydos, on the Asiatic, that the bridge had been built. To reach Abydos, the route was north, through the province of Mysia. In their progress the guides of the army kept well inland, so as to avoid the indentations of the coast, and the various small rivers which here flow westward toward the sea. Thus advancing, the army passed to the right of Mount Ida, and arrived at last on the bank of the Scamander. Here they encamped. They were upon the plain of Troy.

The world was filled, in those days, with the glory of the military exploits which had been performed, some ages before, in the siege and capture of Troy; and it was the custom for every military hero who passed the site of the city to pause in his march and spend some time amid the scenes of those ancient conflicts, that he might inspirit and invigorate his own ambition by the associations of the spot, and also render suitable honors to the memories of those that fell there. Xerxes did this. Alexander subsequently did it. Xerxes examined the various localities, ascended the ruins of the citadel of Priam, walked over the ancient battle fields, and at length, when his curiosity had thus been satisfied, he ordered a grand sacrifice of a thousand oxen to be made, and a libation of corresponding magnitude to be offered, in honor of the shades of the dead heroes whose deeds had consecrated the spot.

Whatever excitement and exhilaration, however, Xerxes himself may have felt, in approaching, under these circumstances, the transit of the stream, where the real labors and dangers of his expedition were to commence, his miserable and helpless soldiers did not share them. Their condition and prospects were wretched in the extreme. In the first place, none of them went willingly. In modern times, at least in England and America, armies are recruited by enticing the depraved and the miserable to enlist, by tendering them a bounty, as it is called, that is, a sum of ready money, which, as a means of temporary and often vicious pleasure, presents a temptation they can not resist. The act of enlistment is, however, in a sense voluntary, so that those who have homes, and friends, and useful pursuits in which they are peacefully engaged, are not disturbed. It was not so with the soldiers of Xerxes. They were slaves, and had been torn from their rural homes all over the empire by a merciless conscription, from which there was no possible escape. Their life in camp, too, was comfortless and wretched. At the present day, when it is so much more difficult than it then was to obtain soldiers, and when so much more time and attention are required to train them to their work in the modern art of war, soldiers must be taken care of when obtained; but in Xerxes's day it was much easier to get new supplies of recruits than to incur any great expense in providing for the health and comfort of those already in the service. The arms and trappings, it is true, of such troops as were in immediate attendance on the king, were very splendid and gay, though this was only decoration, after all, and the king's decoration too, not theirs. In respect, however, to every thing like personal comfort, whether of food and of clothing, or the means of shelter and repose, the common soldiers were utterly destitute and wretched. They felt no interest in the campaign; they had nothing to hope for from its success, but a continuance, if their lives were spared, of the same miserable bondage which they had always endured. There was, however, little probability even of this; for whether, in the case of such an invasion, the aggressor was to succeed or to fail, the destiny of the soldiers personally was almost inevitable destruction. The mass of Xerxes's army was thus a mere herd of slaves, driven along by the whips of their officers, reluctant, wretched, and despairing.

This helpless mass was overtaken one night, among the gloomy and rugged defiles and passes of Mount Ida, by a dreadful storm of wind and rain, accompanied by thunder and lightning. Unprovided as they were with the means of protection against such tempests, they were thrown into confusion, and spent the night in terror. Great numbers perished, struck by the lightning, or exhausted by the cold and exposure; and afterward, when they encamped on the plains of Troy, near the Scamander, the whole of the water of the stream was not enough to supply the wants of the soldiers and the immense herds of beasts of burden, so that many thousands suffered severely from thirst.

All these things conspired greatly to depress the spirits of the men, so that, at last, when they arrived in the vicinity of Abydos, the whole army was in a state of extreme dejection and despair. This, however, was of little consequence. The repose of a master so despotic and lofty as Xerxes is very little disturbed by the mental sorrows of his slaves. Xerxes reached Abydos, and prepared to make the passage of the strait in a manner worthy of the grandeur of the occasion.

The first thing was to make arrangements for a great parade of his forces, not, apparently, for the purpose of accomplishing any useful end of military organization in the arrangement of the troops, but to gratify the pride and pleasure of the sovereign with an opportunity of surveying them. A great white throne of marble was accordingly erected on an eminence not far from the shore of the Hellespont, from which Xerxes looked down with great complacency and pleasure, on the one hand, upon the long lines of troops, the countless squadrons of horsemen, the ranges of tents, and the vast herds of beasts of burden which were assembled on the land, and, on the other hand, upon the fleets of ships, and boats, and galleys at anchor upon the sea; while the shores of Europe were smiling in the distance, and the long and magnificent roadway which he had made lay floating upon the water, all ready to take his enormous armament across whenever he should issue the command.

Any deep emotion of the human soul, in persons of a sensitive physical organization, tends to tears; and Xerxes's heart, being filled with exultation and pride, and with a sense of inexpressible grandeur and sublimity as he looked upon this scene, was softened by the pleasurable excitements of the hour, and though, at first his countenance was beaming with satisfaction and pleasure, his uncle Artabanus, who stood by his side, soon perceived that tears were standing in his eyes. Artabanus asked him what this meant. It made him sad, Xerxes replied, to reflect that, immensely vast as the countless multitude before him was, in one hundred years from that time not one of them all would be alive.

The tender-heartedness which Xerxes manifested on this occasion, taken in connection with the stern and unrelenting tyranny which he was exercising over the mighty mass of humanity whose mortality he mourned, has drawn forth a great variety of comments from writers of every age who have repeated the story. Artabanus replied to it on the spot by saying that he did not think that the king ought to give himself too much uneasiness on the subject of human liability to death, for it happened, in a vast number of cases, that the privations and sufferings of men were so great, that often, in the course of their lives, they rather wished to die than to live; and that death was, consequently, in some respects, to be regarded, not as in itself a woe, but rather as the relief and remedy for woe.

There is no doubt that this theory of Artabanus, so far as it applied to the unhappy soldiers of Xerxes, all marshaled before him when he uttered it, was eminently true.

Xerxes admitted that what his uncle said was just, but it was, he said, a melancholy subject, and so he changed the conversation. He asked his uncle whether he still entertained the same doubts and fears in respect to the expedition that he had expressed at Susa when the plan was first proposed in the council. Artabanus replied that he most sincerely hoped that the prognostications of the vision would prove true, but that he had still great apprehensions of the result. "I have been reflecting," continued he, "with great care on the whole subject, and it seems to me that there are two dangers of very serious character to which your expedition will be imminently exposed."

Xerxes wished to know what they were.

"They both arise," said Artabanus, "from the immense magnitude of your operations. In the first place, you have so large a number of ships, galleys, and transports in your fleet, that I do not see how, when you have gone down upon the Greek coast, if a storm should arise, you are going to find shelter for them. There are no harbors there large enough to afford anchorage ground for such an immense number of vessels."

"And what is the other danger?" asked Xerxes.

"The other is the difficulty of finding food for such a vast multitude of men as you have brought together in your armies. The quantity of food necessary to supply such countless numbers is almost incalculable. Your granaries and magazines will soon be exhausted, and then, as no country whatever that you can pass through will have resources of food adequate for such a multitude of mouths, it seems to me that your march must inevitably end in a famine. The less resistance you meet with, and the further you consequently advance, the worse it will be for you. I do not see how this fatal result can possibly be avoided; and so uneasy and anxious am I on the subject, that I have no rest or peace."

"I admit," said Xerxes, in reply, "that what you say is not wholly unreasonable; but in great undertakings it will never do to take counsel wholly of our fears. I am willing to submit to a very large portion of the evils to which I expose myself on this expedition, rather than not accomplish the end which I have in view. Besides, the most prudent and cautious counsels are not always the best. He who hazards nothing gains nothing. I have always observed that in all the affairs of human life, those who exhibit some enterprise and courage in what they undertake are far more likely to be successful than those who weigh every thing and consider every thing, and will not advance where they can see any remote prospect of danger. If my predecessors had acted on the principles which you recommend, the Persian empire would never have acquired the greatness to which it has now attained. In continuing to act on the same principles which governed them, I confidently expect the same success. We shall conquer Europe, and then return in peace, I feel assured, without encountering the famine which you dread so much, or any other great calamity."

On hearing these words, and observing how fixed and settled the determinations of Xerxes were, Artabanus said no more on the general subject, but on one point he ventured to offer his counsel to his nephew, and that was on the subject of employing the Ionians in the war. The Ionians were Greeks by descent. Their ancestors had crossed the Ægean Sea, and settled at various places along the coast of Asia Minor, in the western part of the provinces of Caria, Lydia, and Mysia. Artabanus thought it was dangerous to take these men to fight against their countrymen. However faithfully disposed they might be in commencing the enterprise, a thousand circumstances might occur to shake their fidelity and lead them to revolt, when they found themselves in the land of their forefathers, and heard the enemies against whom they had been brought to contend speaking their own mother tongue.

Xerxes, however, was not convinced by Artabanus's arguments. He thought that the employment of the Ionians was perfectly safe. They had been eminently faithful and firm, he said, under Histiaeus, in the time of Darius's invasion of Scythia, when Darius had left them to guard his bridge over the Danube. They had proved themselves trustworthy then, and he would, he said, accordingly trust them now. "Besides," he added, "they have left their property, their wives and their children, and all else that they hold dear, in our hands in Asia, and they will not dare, while we retain such hostages, to do any thing against us."

Xerxes said, however, that since Artabanus was so much concerned in respect to the result of the expedition, he should not be compelled to accompany it any further, but that he might return to Susa instead, and take charge of the government there until Xerxes should return.

A part of the celebration on the great day of parade, on which this conversation between the king and his uncle was held, consisted of a naval sea fight, waged on the Hellespont, between two of the nations of his army, for the king's amusement. The Phoenicians were the victors in this combat. Xerxes was greatly delighted with the combat, and, in fact, with the whole of the magnificent spectacle which the day had displayed.

Soon after this, Xerxes dismissed Artabanus, ordering him to return to Susa, and to assume the regency of the empire. He convened, also, another general council of the nobles of his court and the officers of the army, to announce to them that the time had arrived for crossing the bridge, and to make his farewell address to them before they should take their final departure from Asia. He exhorted them to enter upon the great work before them with a determined and resolute spirit, saying that if the Greeks were once subdued, no other enemies able at all to cope with the Persians would be left on the habitable globe.

On the dismission of the council, orders were given to commence the crossing of the bridge the next day at sunrise. The preparations were made accordingly. In the morning, as soon as it was light, and while waiting for the rising of the sun, they burned upon the bridge all manner of perfumes, and strewed the way with branches of myrtle, the emblem of triumph and joy. As the time for the rising of the sun drew nigh, Xerxes stood with a golden vessel full of wine, which he was to pour out as a libation as soon as the first dazzling beams should appear above the horizon. When, at length, the moment arrived, he poured out the wine into the sea, throwing the vessel in which it had been contained after it as an offering. He also threw in, at the same time, a golden goblet of great value, and a Persian cimeter. The ancient historian who records these facts was uncertain whether these offerings were intended as acts of adoration addressed to the sun, or as oblations presented to the sea—a sort of peace offering, perhaps, to soothe the feelings of the mighty monster, irritated and chafed by the chastisement which it had previously received.

Xerxes Crossing the Hellespont.

One circumstance indicated that the offering was intended for the sun, for, at the time of making it, Xerxes addressed to the great luminary a sort of petition, which might be considered either an apostrophe or a prayer, imploring its protection. He called upon the sun to accompany and defend the expedition, and to preserve it from every calamity until it should have accomplished its mission of subjecting all Europe to the Persian sway.

The army then commenced its march. The order of march was very much the same as that which had been observed in the departure from Sardis. The beasts of burden and the baggage were preceded and followed by immense bodies of troops of all nations. The whole of the first day was occupied by the passing of this part of the army. Xerxes himself, and the sacred portion of the train, were to follow them on the second day. Accordingly, there came, on the second day, first, an immense squadron of horse, with garlands on the heads of the horsemen; next, the sacred horses and the sacred car of Jupiter. Then came Xerxes himself, in his war chariot, with trumpets sounding, and banners waving in the air. At the moment when Xerxes's chariot entered upon the bridge, the fleet of galleys, which had been drawn up in preparation near the Asiatic shore, were set in motion, and moved in a long and majestic line across the strait to the European side, accompanying and keeping pace with their mighty master in his progress. Thus was spent the second day.

Five more days were consumed in getting over the remainder of the army, and the immense trains of beasts and of baggage which followed. The officers urged the work forward as rapidly as possible, and, toward the end, as is always the case in the movement of such enormous masses, it became a scene of inconceivable noise, terror, and confusion. The officers drove forward men and beasts alike by the lashes of their whips—every one struggling, under the influence of such stimulants, to get forward—while fallen animals, broken wagons, and the bodies of those exhausted and dying with excitement and fatigue, choked the way. The mighty mass was, however, at last transferred to the European continent, full of anxious fears in respect to what awaited them, but yet having very faint and feeble conceptions of the awful scenes in which the enterprise of their reckless leader was to end.

6

The Review of the Troops at Doriscus

B.C. 480

The fleet and the army separate.—The Chersonesus.—Sufferings from thirst.—The Hebrus.—Plain of Doriscus.—Preparations for the great review.—Mode of taking a census.—Immense numbers of the troops.—The cavalry.—Corps of Arabs and Egyptians.—Sum total of the army.—Various nations.—Dress and equipments.—Uncouth costumes.—Various weapons.—The lasso.—Dresses of various kinds.—The Immortals.—Privileges of the Immortals.—The fleet.—Xerxes reviews the troops.—He reviews the fleet.—A lady admiral.—Her abilities.—Number of vessels in the fleet.—Demaratus the Greek.—Story of Demaratus.—Childhood of his mother.—The change.—Ariston, king of Sparta.—The agreement.—Birth of Demaratus.—Demaratus disowned.—His flight.—Question of Xerxes.—Perplexity of Demaratus.—Demaratus describes the Spartans.—Surprise of Xerxes.—Reply of Xerxes.—His displeasure.—Demaratus's apology.—His gratitude to Darius.—Demaratus's defense of the Spartans.—They are governed by law.—Xerxes resumes his march.—Division of the army.—The Strymon.—Human sacrifices.—Arrival at the canal.—Death of the engineer.—Burial of the engineer.—A grand feast.—Scene of revelry.—Desolation and depopulation of the country.

AS soon as the expedition of Xerxes had crossed the Hellespont and arrived safely on the European side, as narrated in the last chapter, it became necessary for the fleet and the army to separate, and to move, for a time, in opposite directions from each other. The reader will observe, by examining the map, that the army, on reaching the European shore, at the point to which they would be conducted by a bridge at Abydos, would find themselves in the middle of a long and narrow peninsula called the Chersonesus, and that, before commencing its regular march along the northern coast of the Ægean Sea, it would be necessary first to proceed for fifteen or twenty miles to the eastward, in order to get round the bay by which the peninsula is bounded on the north and west. While, therefore, the fleet went directly westward along the coast, the army turned to the eastward, a place of rendezvous having been appointed on the northern coast of the sea, where they were all soon to meet again.

The army moved on by a slow and toilsome progress until it reached the neck of the peninsula, and then turning at the head of the bay, it moved westward again, following the direction of the coast. The line of march was, however, laid at some distance from the shore, partly for the sake of avoiding the indentations made in the land by gulfs and bays, and partly for the sake of crossing the streams from the interior at points so far inland that the water found in them should be fresh and pure. Notwithstanding these precautions, however, the water often failed. So immense were the multitudes of men and of beasts, and so craving was the thirst which the heat and the fatigues of the march engendered, that, in several instances, they drank the little rivers dry.

The first great and important river which the army had to pass after entering Europe was the Hebrus. Not far from the mouth of the Hebrus, where it emptied into the Ægean Sea, was a great plain, which was called the plain of Doriscus. There was an extensive fortress here, which had been erected by the orders of Darius when he had subjugated this part of the country. The position of this fortress was an important one, because it commanded the whole region watered by the Hebrus, which was a very fruitful and populous district. Xerxes had been intending to have a grand review and enumeration of his forces on entering the European territories, and he judged Doriscus to be a very suitable place for his purpose. He could establish his own head-quarters in the fortress, while his armies could be marshaled and reviewed on the plain. The fleet, too, had been ordered to draw up to the shore at the same spot, and when the army reached the ground, they found the vessels already in the offing.

The army accordingly halted, and the necessary arrangements were made for the review. The first thing was to ascertain the numbers of the troops; and as the soldiers were too numerous to be counted, Xerxes determined to measure the mighty mass as so much bulk, and then ascertain the numbers by a computation. They made the measure itself in the following manner: They counted off, first, ten thousand men, and brought them together in a compact circular mass, in the middle of the plain, and then marked a line upon the ground inclosing them. Upon this line, thus determined, they built a stone wall, about four feet high, with openings on opposite sides of it, by which men might enter and go out. When the wall was built, soldiers were sent into the inclosure—just as corn would be poured by a husbandman into a wooden peck—until it was full. The mass thus required to fill the inclosure was deemed and taken to be ten thousand men. This was the first filling of the measure. These men were then ordered to retire, and a fresh mass was introduced, and so on until the whole army was measured. The inclosure was filled one hundred and seventy times with the foot soldiers before the process was completed, indicating, as the total amount of the infantry of the army, a force of one million seven hundred thousand men. This enumeration, it must be remembered, included the land forces alone.

This method of measuring the army in bulk was applied only to the foot soldiers; they constituted the great mass of the forces convened. There were, however, various other bodies of troops in the army, which, from their nature, were more systematically organized than the common foot soldiers, and so their numbers were known by the regular enrollment. There was, for example, a cavalry force of eighty thousand men. There was also a corps of Arabs, on camels, and another of Egyptians, in war chariots, which together amounted to twenty thousand. Then, besides these land forces, there were half a million of men in the fleet. Immense as these numbers are, they were still further increased, as the army moved on, by Xerxes's system of compelling the forces of every kingdom and province through which he passed to join the expedition; so that, at length, when the Persian king fairly entered the heart of the Greek territory, Herodotus, the great narrator of his history, in summing up the whole number of men regularly connected with the army, makes a total of about five millions of men. One hundred thousand men, which is but one fiftieth part of five millions, is considered, in modern times, an immense army; and, in fact, half even of that number was thought, in the time of the American Revolution, a sufficient force to threaten the colonies with overwhelming destruction. "If ten thousand men will not do to put down the rebellion," said an orator in the House of Commons, "fifty thousand shall."

Herodotus adds that, besides the five millions regularly connected with the army, there was an immense and promiscuous mass of women, slaves, cooks, bakers, and camp followers of every description, that no human powers could estimate or number.

But to return to the review. The numbers of the army having been ascertained, the next thing was to marshal and arrange the men by nations under their respective leaders, to be reviewed by the king. A very full enumeration of these divisions of the army is given by the historians of the day, with minute descriptions of the kind of armor which the troops of the several nations wore. There were more than fifty of these nations in all. Some of them were highly civilized, others were semi-barbarous tribes; and, of course, they presented, as marshaled in long array upon the plain, every possible variety of dress and equipment. Some were armed with brazen helmets, and coats of mail formed of plates of iron; others wore linen tunics, or rude garments made of the skins of beasts. The troops of one nation had their heads covered with helmets, those of another with miters, and of a third with tiaras. There was one savage-looking horde that had caps made of the skin of the upper part of a horse's head, in its natural form, with the ears standing up erect at the top, and the mane flowing down behind. These men held the skins of cranes before them instead of shields, so that they looked like horned monsters, half beast and half bird, endeavoring to assume the guise and attitude of men. There was another corps whose men were really horned, since they wore caps made from the skins of the heads of oxen, with the horns standing. Wild beasts were personated, too, as well as tame; for some nations were clothed in lions' skins, and others in panthers' skins—the clothing being considered, apparently, the more honorable, in proportion to the ferocity of the brute to which it had originally belonged.

The weapons, too, were of every possible form and guise. Spears—some pointed with iron, some with stone, and others shaped simply by being burned to a point in the fire; bows and arrows, of every variety of material and form, swords, daggers, slings, clubs, darts, javelins, and every other imaginable species of weapon which human ingenuity, savage or civilized, had then conceived. Even the lasso—the weapon of the American aborigines of modern times—was there. It is described by the ancient historian as a long thong of leather wound into a coil, and finished in a noose at the end, which noose the rude warrior who used the implement launched through the air at the enemy, and entangling rider and horse together by means of it, brought them both to the ground.

There was every variety of taste, too, in the fashion and the colors of the dresses which were worn. Some were of artificial fabrics, and dyed in various and splendid hues. Some were very plain, the wearers of them affecting a simple and savage ferocity in the fashion of their vesture. Some tribes had painted skins—beauty, in their view, consisting, apparently, in hideousness. There was one barbarian horde who wore very little clothing of any kind. They had knotty clubs for weapons, and, in lieu of a dress, they had painted their naked bodies half white and half a bright vermilion.

In all this vast array, the corps which stood at the head, in respect to their rank and the costliness and elegance of their equipment, was a Persian squadron of ten thousand men, called the Immortals. They had received this designation from the fact that the body was kept always exactly full, as, whenever any one of the number died, another soldier was instantly put into his place, whose life was considered in some respects a continuation of the existence of the man who had fallen. Thus, by a fiction somewhat analogous to that by which the king, in England, never dies, these ten thousand Persians were an immortal band. They were all carefully-selected soldiers, and they enjoyed very unusual privileges and honors. They were mounted troops, and their dress and their armor were richly decorated with gold. They were accompanied in their campaigns by their wives and families, for whose use carriages were provided which followed the camp, and there was a long train of camels besides, attached to the service of the corps, to carry their provisions and their baggage.

While all these countless varieties of land troops were marshaling and arranging themselves upon the plain, each under its own officers and around its own standards, the naval commanders were employed in bringing up the fleet of galleys to the shore, where they were anchored in a long line not far from the beach, and with their prows toward the land. Thus there was a space of open water left between the line of vessels and the beach, along which Xerxes's barge was to pass when the time for the naval part of the review should arrive.

When all things were ready, Xerxes mounted his war chariot and rode slowly around the plain, surveying attentively, and with great interest and pleasure, the long lines of soldiers, in all their variety of equipment and costume, as they stood displayed before him. It required a progress of many miles to see them all. When this review of the land forces was concluded, the king went to the shore, and embarked on board a royal galley which had been prepared for him, and there, seated upon the deck under a gilded canopy, he was rowed by the oarsmen along the line of ships, between their prows and the land. The ships were from many nations as well as the soldiers, and exhibited the same variety of fashion and equipment. The land troops had come from the inland realms and provinces which occupied the heart of Asia, while the ships and the seamen had been furnished by the maritime regions which extended along the coasts of the Black, and the Ægean, and the Mediterranean Seas. Thus the people of Egypt had furnished two hundred ships, the Phoenicians three hundred, Cyprus fifty, the Cilicians and the Ionians one hundred each, and so with a great many other nations and tribes.

The various squadrons which were thus combined in forming this immense fleet were manned and officered, of course, from the nations that severally furnished them, and one of them was actually commanded in person by a queen. The name of this lady admiral was Artemisia. She was the Queen of Caria, a small province in the southwestern part of Asia Minor, having Halicarnassus for its capital. Artemisia, though in history called a queen, was, in reality, more properly a regent, as she governed in the name of her son, who was yet a child. The quota of ships which Caria was to furnish was five. Artemisia, being a lady of ambitious and masculine turn of mind, and fond of adventure, determined to accompany the expedition. Not only her own vessels, but also those from some neighboring islands, were placed under her charge, so that she commanded quite an important division of the fleet. She proved, also, in the course of the voyage, to be abundantly qualified for the discharge of her duties. She became, in fact, one of the ablest and most efficient commanders in the fleet, not only maneuvering and managing her own particular division in a very successful manner, but also taking a very active and important part in the general consultations, where what she said was listened to with great respect, and always had great weight in determining the decisions. In the great battle of Salamis she acted a very conspicuous part, as will hereafter appear.

The whole number of galleys of the first class in Xerxes's fleet was more than twelve hundred, a number abundantly sufficient to justify the apprehensions of Artabanus that no harbor would be found capacious enough to shelter them in the event of a sudden storm. The line which they formed on this occasion, when drawn up side by side upon the shore for review, must have extended many miles.

Xerxes moved slowly along this line in his barge, attended by the officers of his court and the great generals of his army, who surveyed the various ships as they passed them, and noted the diverse national costumes and equipments of the men with curiosity and pleasure. Among those who attended the king on this occasion was a certain Greek named Demaratus, an exile from his native land, who had fled to Persia, and had been kindly received by Darius some years before. Having remained in the Persian court until Xerxes succeeded to the throne and undertook the invasion of Greece, he concluded to accompany the expedition.

The story of the political difficulties in which Demaratus became involved in his native land, and which led to his flight from Greece, was very extraordinary. It was this:

The mother of Demaratus was the daughter of parents of high rank and great affluence in Sparta, but in her childhood her features were extremely plain and repulsive. Now there was a temple in the neighborhood of the place where her parents resided, consecrated to Helen, a princess who, while she lived, enjoyed the fame of being the most beautiful woman in the world. The nurse recommended that the child should be taken every day to this temple, and that petitions should be offered there at the shrine of Helen that the repulsive deformity of her features might be removed. The mother consented to this plan, only enjoining upon the nurse not to let any one see the face of her unfortunate offspring in going and returning. The nurse accordingly carried the child to the temple day after day, and holding it in her arms before the shrine, implored the mercy of Heaven for her helpless charge, and the bestowal upon it of the boon of beauty.

These petitions were, it seems, at length heard, for one day, when the nurse was coming down from the temple, after offering her customary prayer, she was met and accosted by a mysterious-looking woman, who asked her what it was that she was carrying in her arms. The nurse replied that it was a child. The woman wanted to look at it. The nurse refused to show the face of the child, saying that she had been forbidden to do so. The woman, however, insisted upon seeing its face, and at last the nurse consented and removed the coverings. The stranger stroked down the face of the child, saying, at the same time, that now that child should become the most beautiful woman of Sparta.

Her words proved true. The features of the young girl rapidly changed, and her countenance soon became as wonderful for its loveliness as it had been before for its hideous deformity. When she arrived at a proper age, a certain Spartan nobleman named Agetus, a particular friend of the king's, made her his wife.

The name of the king of Sparta at that time was Ariston. He had been twice married, and his second wife was still living, but he had no children. When he came to see and to know the beautiful wife of Agetus, he wished to obtain her for himself, and began to revolve the subject in his mind, with a view to discover some method by which he might hope to accomplish his purpose. He decided at length upon the following plan. He proposed to Agetus to make an exchange of gifts, offering to give to him any one object which he might choose from all his, that is, Ariston's effects, provided that Agetus would, in the same manner, give to Ariston whatever Ariston might choose. Agetus consented to the proposal, without, however, giving it any serious consideration. As Ariston was already married, he did not for a moment imagine that his wife could be the object which the king would demand. The parties to this foolish agreement confirmed the obligation of it by a solemn oath, and then each made known to the other what he had selected. Agetus gained some jewel, or costly garment, or perhaps a gilded and embellished weapon, and lost forever his beautiful wife. Ariston repudiated his own second wife, and put the prize which he had thus surreptitiously acquired in her place as a third.

About seven or eight months after this time Demaratus was born. The intelligence was brought to Ariston one day by a slave, when he was sitting at a public tribunal. Ariston seemed surprised at the intelligence, and exclaimed that the child was not his. He, however, afterward retracted this disavowal, and owned Demaratus as his son. The child grew up, and in process of time, when his father died, he succeeded to the throne. The magistrates, however, who had heard the declaration of his father at the time of his birth, remembered it, and reported it to others; and when Ariston died and Demaratus assumed the supreme power, the next heir denied his right to the succession, and in process of time formed a strong party against him. A long series of civil dissensions arose, and at length the claims of Demaratus were defeated, his enemies triumphed, and he fled from the country to save his life. He arrived at Susa near the close of Darius's reign, and it was his counsel which led the king to decide the contest among his sons for the right of succession, in favor of Xerxes, as described at the close of the first chapter. Xerxes had remembered his obligations to Demaratus for this interposition. He had retained him in the royal court after his accession to the throne, and had bestowed upon him many marks of distinction and honor.

Demaratus had decided to accompany Xerxes on his expedition into Greece, and now, while the Persian officers were looking with so much pride and pleasure on the immense preparations which they were making for the subjugation of a foreign and hostile state, Demaratus, too, was in the midst of the scene, regarding the spectacle with no less of interest, probably, and yet, doubtless, with very different feelings, since the country upon which this dreadful cloud of gloom and destruction was about to burst was his own native land.

After the review was ended, Xerxes sent for Demaratus to come to the castle. When he arrived, the king addressed him as follows:

"You are a Greek, Demaratus, and you know your countrymen well; and now, as you have seen the fleet and the army that have been displayed here to-day, tell me what is your opinion. Do you think that the Greeks will undertake to defend themselves against such a force, or will they submit at once without attempting any resistance?"

Demaratus seemed at first perplexed and uncertain, as if not knowing exactly what answer to make to the question. At length he asked the king whether it was his wish that he should respond by speaking the blunt and honest truth, or by saying what would be polite and agreeable.

Xerxes replied that he wished him, of course, to speak the truth. The truth itself would be what he should consider the most agreeable.

"Since you desire it, then," said Demaratus, "I will speak the exact truth. Greece is the child of poverty. The inhabitants of the land have learned wisdom and discipline in the severe school of adversity, and their resolution and courage are absolutely indomitable. They all deserve this praise; but I speak more particularly of my own countrymen, the people of Sparta. I am sure that they will reject any proposal which you may make to them for submission to your power, and that they will resist you to the last extremity. The disparity of numbers will have no influence whatever on their decision. If all the rest of Greece were to submit to you, leaving the Spartans alone, and if they should find themselves unable to muster more than a thousand men, they would give you battle."

Xerxes expressed great surprise at this assertion, and thought that Demaratus could not possibly mean what he seemed to say. "I appeal to yourself," said he; "would you dare to encounter, alone, ten men? You have been the prince of the Spartans, and a prince ought, at least, to be equal to two common men; so that to show that the Spartans in general could be brought to fight a superiority of force of even ten to one, it ought to appear that you would dare to engage twenty. This is manifestly absurd. In fact, for any person to pretend to be able or willing to fight under such a disparity of numbers, evinces only pride and insolent presumption. And even this proportion of ten to one, or even twenty to one, is nothing compared to the real disparity; for, even if we grant to the Spartans as large a force as there is any possibility of their obtaining, I shall then have a thousand to one against them.

"Besides," continued the king, "there is a great difference in the character of the troops. The Greeks are all freemen, while my soldiers are all slaves—bound absolutely to do my bidding, without complaint or murmur. Such soldiers as mine, who are habituated to submit entirely to the will of another, and who live under the continual fear of the lash, might, perhaps, be forced to go into battle against a great superiority of numbers, or under other manifest disadvantages; but free men, never. I do not believe that a body of Greeks could be brought to engage a body of Persians, man for man. Every consideration shows, thus, that the opinion which you have expressed is unfounded. You could only have been led to entertain such an opinion through ignorance and unaccountable presumption."

"I was afraid," replied Demaratus, "from the first, that, by speaking the truth, I should offend you. I should not have given you my real opinion of the Spartans if you had not ordered me to speak without reserve. You certainly can not suppose me to have been influenced by a feeling of undue partiality for the men whom I commended, since they have been my most implacable and bitter enemies, and have driven me into hopeless exile from my native land. Your father, on the other hand, received and protected me, and the sincere gratitude which I feel for the favors which I have received from him and from you incline me to take the most favorable view possible of the Persian cause.

"I certainly should not be willing, as you justly suppose, to engage, alone, twenty men, or ten, or even one, unless there was an absolute necessity for it. I do not say that any single Lacedaemonian could successfully encounter ten or twenty Persians, although in personal conflicts they are certainly not inferior to other men. It is when they are combined in a body even though that body be small, that their great superiority is seen.

"As to their being free, and thus not easily led into battle in circumstances of imminent danger, it must be considered that their freedom is not absolute, like that of savages in a fray, where each acts according to his own individual will and pleasure, but it is qualified and controlled by law. The Spartan soldiers are not personal slaves, governed by the lash of a master, it is true; but they have certain principles of obligation and duty which they all feel most solemnly bound to obey. They stand in greater awe of the authority of this law than your subjects do of the lash. It commands them never to fly from the field of battle, whatever may be the number of their adversaries. It commands them to preserve their ranks, to stand firm at the posts assigned them, and there to conquer or die.

"This is the truth in respect to them. If what I say seems to you absurd, I will in future be silent. I have spoken honestly what I think, because your majesty commanded me to do so; and, notwithstanding what I have said, I sincerely wish that all your majesty's desires and expectations may be fulfilled."

The ideas which Demaratus thus appeared to entertain of danger to the countless and formidable hosts of Xerxes's army, from so small and insignificant a power as that of Sparta, seemed to Xerxes too absurd to awaken any serious displeasure in his mind. He only smiled, therefore, at Demaratus's fears, and dismissed him.

Leaving a garrison and a governor in possession of the castle of Doriscus, Xerxes resumed his march along the northern shores of the Ægean Sea, the immense swarms of men filling all the roads, devouring every thing capable of being used as food, either for beast or man, and drinking all the brooks and smaller rivers dry. Even with this total consumption of the food and the water which they obtained on the march, the supplies would have been found insufficient if the whole army had advanced through one tract of country. They accordingly divided the host into three great columns, one of which kept near the shore; the other marched far in the interior, and the third in the intermediate space. They thus exhausted the resources of a very wide region. All the men, too, that were capable of bearing arms in the nations that these several divisions passed on the way, they compelled to join them, so that the army left, as it moved along, a very broad extent of country trampled down, impoverished, desolate, and full of lamentation and woe. The whole march was perhaps the most gigantic crime against the rights and the happiness of man that human wickedness has ever been able to commit.

The army halted, from time to time, for various purposes, sometimes for the performance of what they considered religions ceremonies, which were intended to propitiate the supernatural powers of the earth and of the air. When they reached the Strymon, where, it will be recollected, a bridge had been previously built, so as to be ready for the army when it should arrive, they offered a sacrifice of five white horses to the river. In the same region, too, they halted at a place called the Nine Ways, where Xerxes resolved to offer a human sacrifice to a certain god whom the Persians believed to reside in the interior of the earth. The mode of sacrificing to this god was to bury the wretched victims alive. The Persians seized, accordingly, by Xerxes's orders, nine young men and nine girls from among the people of the country, and buried them alive!

Marching slowly on in this manner, the army at length reached the point upon the coast where the canal had been cut across the isthmus of Mount Athos. The town which was nearest to this spot was Acanthus, the situation of which, together with that of the canal, will be found upon the map. The fleet arrived at this point by sea nearly at the same time with the army coming by land. Xerxes examined the canal, and was extremely well satisfied with its construction. He commended the chief engineer, whose name was Artachaees, in the highest terms, for the successful manner in which he had executed the work, and rendered him very distinguished honors.

It unfortunately happened, however, that, a few days after the arrival of the fleet and the army at the canal, and before the fleet had commenced the passage of it, that Artachaees died. The king considered this event as a serious calamity to him, as he expected that other occasions would arrive on which he would have occasion to avail himself of the engineer's talents and skill. He ordered preparations to be made for a most magnificent burial, and the body was in due time deposited in the grave with imposing funeral solemnities. A very splendid monument, too, was raised upon the spot, which employed, for some time, all the mechanical force of the army in its erection.

While Xerxes remained at Acanthus, he required the people of the neighboring country to entertain his army at a grand feast, the cost of which totally ruined them. Not only was all the food of the vicinity consumed, but all the means and resources of the inhabitants, of every kind, were exhausted in the additional supplies which they had to procure from the surrounding regions. At this feast the army in general ate, seated in groups upon the ground, in the open air; but for Xerxes and the nobles of the court a great pavilion was built, where tables were spread, and vessels and furniture of silver and gold, suitable to the dignity of the occasion, were provided. Almost all the property which the people of the region had accumulated by years of patient industry was consumed at once in furnishing the vast amount of food which was required for this feast, and the gold and silver plate which was to be used in the pavilion. During the entertainment, the inhabitants of the country waited upon their exacting and insatiable guests until they were utterly exhausted by the fatigues of the service. When, at length, the feast was ended, and Xerxes and his company left the pavilion, the vast assembly outside broke up in disorder, pulled the pavilion to pieces, plundered the tables of the gold and silver plate, and departed to their several encampments, leaving nothing behind them.

The inhabitants of the country were so completely impoverished and ruined by these exactions, that those who were not impressed into Xerxes's service and compelled to follow his army, abandoned their homes, and roamed away in the hope of finding elsewhere the means of subsistence which it was no longer possible to obtain on their own lands; and thus, when Xerxes at last gave orders to the fleet to pass through the canal, and to his army to resume its march, he left the whole region utterly depopulated and desolate.

He went on to Therma, a port situated on the northwestern corner of the Ægean Sea, which was the last of his places of rendezvous before his actual advance into Greece.

7

The Preparations of the Greeks for Defense

B.C. 480

The Greeks.—The two prominent states of Greece.—Greek kings.—The two kings of Sparta.—Origin of the custom of two kings.—The twins.—The Delphic oracle consulted.—Plan for ascertaining the eldest.—Civil dissensions.—Two lines established.—Character of the Spartans.—Their lofty spirit.—The Athenians.—The city of Athens.—Sparta and Athens defy the Persians.—Earth and water.—Spirit of the Spartans.—The blank tablets.—Leonidas.—His wife discovers the writing on the tablets. —The three spies.—Alarm at Athens.—The Greeks consult the Delphic oracle.—The responses.—Various interpretations of the oracle.—The Athenian fleet.—Themistocles.—Proposed confederation.—Council of Spartans and Athenians.—The Argives reject the propositions of the Spartans. —Embassy to Sicily.—Demands of Gelon.—The embassadors go to Corcyra.—The River Peneus.—The Vale of Tempe.—Straits of Thermopylae. —Question to be decided.—Messengers from Thessaly.—Negotiations.— Decision to defend the Olympic Straits.—Sailing of the fleet.—Advice of the King of Macedon.—The Greeks fall back to Thermopylae.—Xerxes visits Thessaly.—Beautiful rural scene.—Conversation of Xerxes at the Olympic Pass.

WE must now leave, for a time, the operations of Xerxes and his army, and turn our attention to the Greeks, and to the preparations which they were making to meet the emergency.

The two states of Greece which were most prominent in the transactions connected with the invasion of Xerxes were Athens and Sparta. By referring to the map, Athens will be found to have been situated upon a promontory just without the Peloponnesus, while Sparta, on the other hand, was in the center of a valley which lay in the southern part of the peninsula. Each of these cities was the center and strong-hold of a small but very energetic and powerful commonwealth. The two states were entirely independent of each other, and each had its own peculiar system of government, of usages, and of laws. These systems, and, in fact, the characters of the two communities, in all respects, were extremely dissimilar.

Both these states, though in name republics, had certain magistrates, called commonly, in history, kings. These kings were, however, in fact, only military chieftains, commanders of the armies rather than sovereign rulers of the state. The name by which such a chieftain was actually called by the people themselves, in those days, was tyrannus, the name from which our word tyrant is derived. As, however, the word tyrannus had none of that opprobrious import which is associated with its English derivative, the latter is not now a suitable substitute for the former. Historians, therefore, commonly use the word king instead, though that word does not properly express the idea. They were commanders, chieftains, hereditary generals, but not strictly kings. We shall, however, often call them kings, in these narratives, in conformity with the general usage. Demaratus, who had fled from Sparta to seek refuge with Darius, and who was now accompanying Xerxes on his march to Greece, was one of these kings.

It was a peculiarity in the constitution of Sparta that, from a very early period of its history, there had been always two kings, who had held the supreme command in conjunction with each other, like the

Roman consuls in later times. This custom was sustained partly by the idea that by this division of the executive power of the state, the exercise of the power was less likely to become despotic or tyrannical. It had its origin, however, according to the ancient legends, in the following singular occurrences:

At a very early period in the history of Sparta, when the people had always been accustomed, like other states, to have one prince or chieftain, a certain prince died, leaving his wife, whose name was Argia, and two infant children, as his survivors. The children were twins, and the father had died almost immediately after they were born. Now the office of king was in a certain sense hereditary, and yet not absolutely so; for the people were accustomed to assemble on the death of the king, and determine who should be his successor, choosing always, however, the oldest son of the former monarch, unless there was some very extraordinary and imperious reason for not doing so. In this case they decided, as usual, that the oldest son should be king.

But here a very serious difficulty arose, which was, to determine which of the twins was the oldest son. They resembled each other so closely that no stranger could distinguish one from the other at all. The mother said that she could not distinguish them, and that she did not know which was the first-born. This was not strictly true; for she did, in fact, know, and only denied her power to decide the question because she wished to have both of her children kings.

In this perplexity the Spartans sent to the oracle at Delphi to know what they were to do. The oracle gave, as usual, an ambiguous and unsatisfactory response. It directed the people to make both the children kings, but to render the highest honors to the first-born. When this answer was reported at Sparta, it only increased the difficulty; for how were they to render peculiar honors to the first-born unless they could ascertain which the first-born was?

In this dilemma, some person suggested to the magistrates that perhaps Argia really knew which was the eldest child, and that if so, by watching her, to see whether she washed and fed one, uniformly, before the other, or gave it precedence in any other way, by which her latent maternal instinct or partiality might appear, the question might possibly be determined. This plan was accordingly adopted. The magistrates contrived means to place a servant maid in the house to watch the mother in the way proposed, and the result was that the true order of birth was revealed. From that time forward, while they were both considered as princes, the one now supposed to be the first-born took precedence of the other.

When, however, the children arrived at an age to assume the exercise of the governmental power, as there was no perceptible difference between them in age, or strength, or accomplishments, the one who had been decided to be the younger was little disposed to submit to the other. Each had his friends and adherents, parties were formed, and a long and angry civil dissension ensued. In the end the question was compromised, the command was divided, and the system of having two chief magistrates became gradually established, the power descending in two lines, from father to son, through many generations. Of course there was perpetual jealousy and dissension, and often open and terrible conflicts, between these two rival lines.

The Spartans were an agricultural people, cultivating the valley in the southeastern part of the Peloponnesus, the waters of which were collected and conveyed to the sea by the River Eurotas and its branches. They lived in the plainest possible manner, and prided themselves on the stern and stoical resolution with which they rejected all the refinements and luxuries of society. Courage, hardihood, indifference to life, and the power to endure without a murmur the most severe and protracted sufferings, were the qualities which they valued. They despised wealth just as other nations despise effeminacy and foppery. Their laws discouraged commerce, lest it should make some of the people rich. Their clothes were scanty and plain, their houses were comfortless, their food was a coarse bread, hard and brown, and their money was of iron. With all this, however, they were the most ferocious and terrible soldiers in the world.

They were, moreover, with all their plainness of manners and of life, of a very proud and lofty spirit. All agricultural toil, and every other species of manual labor in their state, were performed by a servile peasantry, while the free citizens, whose profession was exclusively that of arms, were as aristocratic and exalted in soul as any nobles on earth. People are sometimes, in our day, when money is so much valued, proud, notwithstanding their poverty. The Spartans were proud of their poverty itself. They could be rich if they chose, but they despised riches. They looked down on all the refinements and delicacies of dress and of living from an elevation far above them. They looked down on labor, too, with the same contempt. They were yet very nice and particular about their dress and military appearance, though every thing pertaining to both was coarse and simple, and they had slaves to wait upon them even in their campaigns.

The Athenians were a totally different people. The leading classes in their commonwealth were cultivated, intellectual, and refined. The city of Athens was renowned for the splendor of its architecture, its temples, its citadels, its statues, and its various public institutions, which in subsequent times made it the great intellectual center of Europe. It was populous and wealthy. It had a great commerce and a powerful fleet. The Spartan character, in a word, was stern, gloomy, indomitable, and wholly unadorned. The Athenians were rich, intellectual, and refined. The two nations were nearly equal in power, and were engaged in a perpetual and incessant rivalry.

There were various other states and cities in Greece, but Athens and Sparta were at this time the most considerable, and they were altogether the most resolute and determined in their refusal to submit to the Persian sway. In fact, so well known and understood was the spirit of defiance with which these two powers were disposed to regard the Persian invasion, that when Xerxes sent his summons demanding submission, to the other states of Greece, he did not send any to these. When Darius invaded Greece some years before, he had summoned Athens and Sparta as well as the others, but his demands were indignantly rejected. It seems that the custom was for a government or a prince, when acknowledging the dominion of a superior power, to send, as a token of territorial submission, a little earth and water, which was a sort of legal form of giving up possession of their country to the sovereign who claimed it. Accordingly, when Darius sent his embassadors into Greece to summon the country to surrender, the embassadors, according to the usual form, called upon the governments of the several states to send earth and water to the king. The Athenians, as has been already said, indignantly refused to comply with this demand. The Spartans, not content with a simple refusal, seized the embassadors and threw them into a well, telling them, as they went down, that if they wanted earth and water for the King of Persia, they might get it there.

Fate of the Persian Embassadors at Sparta.

The Greeks had obtained some information of Xerxes's designs against them before they received his summons. The first intelligence was communicated to the Spartans by Demaratus himself, while he was at Susa, in the following singular manner. It was the custom, in those days, to write with a steel point on a smooth surface of wax. The wax was spread for this purpose on a board or tablet of metal, in a very thin stratum, forming a ground upon which the letters traced with the point were easily legible. Demaratus took two writing-tablets such as these, and removing the wax from them, he wrote a brief account of the proposed Persian invasion, by tracing the characters upon the surface of the wood or metal itself, beneath; then, restoring the wax so as to conceal the letters, he sent the two tablets, seemingly blank, to Leonidas, king of Sparta. The messengers who bore them had other pretexts for their journey, and they had various other articles to carry. The Persian guards who stopped and examined the messengers from time to time along the route, thought nothing of the blank tablets, and so they reached Leonidas in safety.

Leonidas being a blunt, rough soldier, and not much accustomed to cunning contrivances himself, was not usually much upon the watch for them from others, and when he saw no obvious communication upon the tablets, he threw them aside, not knowing what the sending of them could mean, and not feeling any strong interest in ascertaining. His wife, however—her name was Gorgo—had more curiosity. There was something mysterious about the affair, and she wished to solve it. She examined the tablets attentively in every part, and at length removed cautiously a little of the wax. The letters began to appear. Full of excitement and pleasure, she proceeded with the work until the whole cereous coating was removed. The result was, that the communication was revealed, and Greece received the warning.

When the Greeks heard that Xerxes was at Sardis, they sent three messengers in disguise, to ascertain the facts in respect to the Persian army assembled there, and, so far as possible, to learn the plans and designs of the king. Notwithstanding all the efforts of these men to preserve their concealment and disguise, they were discovered, seized, and tortured by the Persian officer who took them, until they confessed that they were spies. The officer was about to put them to death, when Xerxes himself received information of the circumstances. He forbade the execution, and directed, on the other hand, that the men should be conducted through all his encampments, and be allowed to view and examine every thing. He then dismissed them, with orders to return to Greece and report what they had seen. He thought, he said, that the Greeks would be more likely to surrender if they knew how immense his preparations were for effectually vanquishing them if they attempted resistance.

The city of Athens, being farther north than Sparta, would be the one first exposed to danger from the invasion, and when the people heard of Xerxes's approach, the whole city was filled with anxiety and alarm. Some of the inhabitants were panic-stricken, and wished to submit; others were enraged, and uttered nothing but threats and defiance. A thousand different plans of defense were proposed and eagerly discussed. At length the government sent messengers to the oracle at Delphi, to learn what their destiny was to be, and to obtain, if possible, divine direction in respect to the best mode of averting the danger. The messengers received an awful response, portending, in wild and solemn, though dark and mysterious language, the most dreadful calamities to the ill-fated city. The messengers were filled with alarm at hearing this reply. One of the inhabitants of Delphi, the city in which the oracle was situated, proposed to them to make a second application, in the character of the most humble supplicants, and to implore that the oracle would give them some directions in respect to the best course for them to pursue in order to avoid, or, at least, to mitigate the impending danger. They did so, and after a time they received an answer, vague, mysterious, and almost unintelligible, but which seemed to denote that the safety of the city was connected in some manner with Salamis, and with certain "wooden walls," to which the inspired distich of the response obscurely alluded.

The messengers returned to Athens and reported the answer which they had received. The people were puzzled and perplexed in their attempts to understand it. It seems that the citadel of Athens had been formerly surrounded by a wooden palisade. Some thought that this was what was referred to by the "wooden walls," and that the meaning of the oracle was that they must rebuild the palisade, and then retreat to the citadel when the Persians should approach, and defend themselves there.

Others conceived that the phrase referred to ships, and that the oracle meant to direct them to meet their enemies with a fleet upon the sea. Salamis, which was also mentioned by the oracle, was an island not far from Athens, being west of the city, between it and the Isthmus of Corinth. Those who supposed that by the "wooden walls" was denoted the fleet, thought that Salamis might have been alluded to as the place near which the great naval battle was to be fought. This was the interpretation which seemed finally to prevail.

The Athenians had a fleet of about two hundred galleys. These vessels had been purchased and built, some time before this, for the Athenian government, through the influence of a certain public officer of high rank and influence, named Themistocles. It seems that a large sum had accumulated in the public treasury, the produce of certain mines belonging to the city, and a proposal was made to divide it among the citizens, which would have given a small sum to each man. Themistocles opposed this proposition, and urged instead that the government should build and equip a fleet with the money. This plan was finally adopted. The fleet was built, and it was now determined to call it into active service to meet and repel the Persians, though the naval armament of Xerxes was six times as large.

The next measure was to establish a confederation, if possible, of the Grecian states, or at least of all those who were willing to combine, and thus to form an allied army to resist the invader. The smaller states were very generally panic-stricken, and had either already signified their submission to the Persian rule, or were timidly hesitating, in doubt whether it would be safer for them to submit to the overwhelming force which was advancing against them, or to join the Athenians and the Spartans in their almost desperate attempts to resist it. The Athenians and Spartans settled, for the time, their own quarrels, and held a council to take the necessary measures for forming a more extended confederation.

All this took place while Xerxes was slowly advancing from Sardis to the Hellespont, and from the Hellespont to Doriscus, as described in the preceding chapter.

The council resolved on dispatching an embassy at once to all the states of Greece, as well as to some of the remoter neighboring powers, asking them to join the alliance.

The first Greek city to which these embassadors came was Argos, which was the capital of a kingdom or state lying between Athens and Sparta, though within the Peloponnesus. The states of Argos and of Sparta, being neighbors, had been constantly at war. Argos had recently lost six thousand men in a battle with the Spartans, and were, consequently, not likely to be in a very favorable mood for a treaty of friendship and alliance.

When the embassadors had delivered their message, the Argolians replied that they had anticipated such a proposal from the time that they had heard that Xerxes had commenced his march toward Greece, and that they had applied, accordingly, to the oracle at Delphi, to know what it would be best for them to do in case the proposal were made. The answer of the oracle had been, they said, unfavorable to their entering into an alliance with the Greeks. They were willing, however, they added, notwithstanding this, to enter into an alliance, offensive and defensive, with the Spartans, for thirty years, on condition that they should themselves have the command of half the Peloponnesian troops. They were entitled to the command of the whole, being, as they contended, the superior nation in rank, but they would waive their just claim, and be satisfied with half, if the Spartans would agree to that arrangement.

The Spartans replied that they could not agree to those conditions. They were themselves, they said, the superior nation in rank, and entitled to the whole command; and as they had two kings, and Argos but one, there was a double difficulty in complying with the Argive demand. They could not surrender one half of the command without depriving one of their kings of his rightful power.

Thus the proposed alliance failed entirely, the people of Argos saying that they would as willingly submit to the dominion of Xerxes as to the insolent demands and assumptions of superiority made by the government of Sparta.

The embassadors among other countries which they visited in their attempts to obtain alliance and aid, went to Sicily. Gelon was the King of Sicily, and Syracuse was his capital. Here the same difficulty occurred which had broken up the negotiations at Argos. The embassadors, when they arrived at Syracuse, represented to Gelon that, if the Persians subdued Greece, they would come to Sicily next, and that it was better for him and for his countrymen that they should meet the enemy while he was still at a distance, rather than to wait until he came near. Gelon admitted the justice of this reasoning, and said that he would furnish a large force, both of ships and men, for carrying on the war, provided that he might have the command of the combined army. To this, of course, the Spartans would not agree. He then asked that he might command the fleet, on condition of giving up his claim to the land forces. This proposition the Athenian embassadors rejected, saying to Gelon that what they were in need of, and came to him to obtain, was a supply of troops, not of leaders. The Athenians, they said, were to command the fleet, being not only the most ancient nation of Greece, but also the most immediately exposed to the invasion, so that they were doubly entitled to be considered as the principals and leaders in the war.

Gelon then told the embassadors that, since they wished to obtain every thing and to concede nothing, they had better leave his dominions without delay, and report to their countrymen that they had nothing to expect from Sicily.

The embassadors went then to Corcyra, a large island on the western coast of Greece, in the Adriatic Sea. It is now called Corfu. Here they seemed to meet with their first success. The people of Corcyra acceded to the proposals made to them, and promised at once to equip and man their fleet, and send it round into the Ægean Sea. They immediately engaged in the work, and seemed to be honestly intent on fulfilling their promises. They were, however, in fact, only pretending. They were really undecided which cause to espouse, the Greek or the Persian, and kept their promised squadron back by means of various delays, until its aid was no longer needed.

But the most important of all these negotiations of the Athenians and Spartans with the neighboring states were those opened with Thessaly. Thessaly was a kingdom in the northern part of Greece. It was, therefore, the territory which the Persian armies would first enter, on turning the northwestern corner of the Ægean Sea. There were, moreover, certain points in its geographical position, and in the physical conformation of the country, that gave it a peculiar importance in respect to the approaching conflict.

By referring to the map placed at the commencement of the fifth chapter, it will be seen that Thessaly was a vast valley, surrounded on all sides by mountainous land, and drained by the River Peneus and its branches. The Peneus flows eastwardly to the Ægean Sea, and escapes from the great valley through a narrow and romantic pass lying between the Mountains Olympus and Ossa. This pass was called in ancient times the Olympic Straits, and a part of it formed a romantic and beautiful glen called the Vale of Tempe. There was a road through this pass, which was the only access by which Thessaly could be entered from the eastward.

To the south of the Vale of Tempe, the mountains, as will appear from the map, crowded so hard upon the sea as not to allow any passage to the eastward of them. The natural route of Xerxes, therefore, in descending into Greece, would be to come down along the coast until he reached the mouth of the Peneus, and then, following the river up through the Vale of Tempe into Thessaly, to pass down toward the Peloponnesus on the western side of Ossa and Pelion, and of the other mountains near the sea. If he could get through the Olympic Straits and the Vale of Tempe, the way would be open and unobstructed until he should reach the southern frontier of Thessaly, where there was another narrow pass leading from Thessaly into Greece. This last defile was close to the sea, and was called the Straits of Thermopylae.

Thus Xerxes and his hosts, in continuing their march to the southward, must necessarily traverse Thessaly, and in doing so they would have two narrow and dangerous defiles to pass—one at Mount Olympus, to get into the country, and the other at Thermopylae, to get out of it. It consequently became a point of great importance to the Greeks to determine at which of these two passes they should make their stand against the torrent which was coming down upon them.

This question would, of course, depend very much upon the disposition of Thessaly herself. The government of that country, understanding the critical situation in which they were placed, had not waited for the Athenians and Spartans to send embassadors to them, but, at a very early period of the war—before, in fact, Xerxes had yet crossed the Hellespont, had sent messengers to Athens to concert some plan of action. These messengers were to say to the Athenians that the government of Thessaly were expecting every day to receive a summons from Xerxes, and that they must speedily decide what they were to do; that they themselves were very unwilling to submit to him, but they could not undertake to make a stand against his immense host alone; that the southern Greeks might include Thessaly in their plan of defense, or exclude it, just as they thought best. If they decided to include it, then they must make a stand at the Olympic Straits, that is, at the pass between Olympus and Ossa; and to do that, it would be necessary to send a strong force immediately to take possession of the pass. If, on the contrary, they decided not to defend Thessaly, then the pass of Thermopylae would be the point at which they must make their stand, and in that case Thessaly must be at liberty to submit on the first Persian summons.

The Greeks, after consultation on the subject, decided that it would be best for them to defend Thessaly, and to take their stand, accordingly, at the Straits of Olympus. They immediately put a large force on board their fleet, armed and equipped for the expedition. This was at the time when Xerxes was just about crossing the Hellespont. The fleet sailed from the port of Athens, passed up through the narrow strait called Euripus, lying between the island of Euboea and the main land, and finally landed at a favorable point of disembarkation, south of Thessaly. From this point the forces marched to the northward until they reached the Peneus, and then established themselves at the narrowest part of the passage between the mountains, strengthened their position there as much as possible, and awaited the coming of the enemy. The amount of the force was ten thousand men.

They had not been here many days before a messenger came to them from the King of Macedon, which country, it will be seen, lies immediately north of Thessaly, earnestly dissuading them from attempting to make a stand at the Vale of Tempe. Xerxes was coming on, he said, with an immense and overwhelming force, one against which it would be utterly impossible for them to make good their defense at such a point as that. It would be far better for them to fall back to Thermopylae, which, being a narrower and more rugged pass, could be more easily defended.

Besides this, the messenger said that it was possible for Xerxes to enter Thessaly without going through the Vale of Tempe at all. The country between Thessaly and Macedon was mountainous, but it was not impassable, and Xerxes would very probably come by that way. The only security, therefore, for the Greeks, would be to fall back and intrench themselves at Thermopylae. Nor was there any time to be lost. Xerxes was crossing the Hellespont, and the whole country was full of excitement and terror.

The Greeks determined to act on this advice. They broke up their encampment at the Olympic Straits, and, retreating to the southward, established themselves at Thermopylae, to await there the coming of the conqueror. The people of Thessaly then surrendered to Xerxes as soon as they received his summons.

Xerxes, from his encampment at Therma, where we left him at the close of the last chapter, saw the peaks of Olympus and Ossa in the southern horizon. They were distant perhaps fifty miles from where he stood. He inquired about them, and was told that the River Peneus flowed between them to the sea, and that through the same defile there lay the main entrance to Thessaly. He had previously determined to march his army round the other way, as the King of Macedon had suggested, but he said that he should like to see this defile. So he ordered a swift Sidonian galley to be prepared, and, taking with him suitable guides, and a fleet of other vessels in attendance on his galley, he sailed to the mouth of the Peneus, and, entering that river, he ascended it until he came to the defile.

Seen from any of the lower elevations which projected from the bases of the mountains at the head of this defile, Thessaly lay spread out before the eye as one vast valley—level, verdant, fertile, and bounded by distant groups and ranges of mountains, which formed a blue and beautiful horizon on every side. Through the midst of this scene of rural loveliness the Peneus, with its countless branches, gracefully meandered, gathering the water from every part of the valley, and then pouring it forth in a deep and calm current through the gap in the mountains at the observer's feet. Xerxes asked his guides if it would be possible to find any other place where the waters of the Peneus could be conducted to the sea. They replied that it would not be, for the valley was bounded on every side by ranges of mountainous land.

"Then," said Xerxes, "the Thessalians were wise in submitting at once to my summons; for, if they had not done so, I would have raised a vast embankment across the valley here, and thus stopped the river, turned their country into a lake, and drowned them all."

8

The Advance of Xerxes into Greece

B.C. 480

Advance of the army.—Sailing of the fleet.—Sciathus.—Euboea.—Straits of Artemisium and Euripus.—Attica.—Saronic Gulf.—Island of Salamis.—Excitement of the country.—Signals.—Sentinels.—Movement of the fleet.—The ten reconnoitering galleys.—Guard-ships captured.—Barbarous ceremony.—A heroic Greek.—One crew escape.—The alarm spread.—Return of the Persian galleys.—The monument of stones.—Progress of the fleet.—The fleet anchors in a bay.—A coming storm.—The storm rages.—Destruction of many vessels.—Plunder of the wrecks.—Scyllias, the famous diver.—Dissensions in the Greek fleet.—Jealousy of the Athenians.—Situation of the Athenians.—Eurybiades appointed commander.—Debates in the Greek council.—Dismay of the Euboeans.—The Greek leaders bribed.—Precautions of the Persians.—Designs of the Persians discovered.—The Greeks decide to give battle.—Euripus and Artemisium.—Advance of the Greeks.—The battle.—A stormy night.—Scene of terror.—A calm after the storm.—Terror of the Euboeans.—Their plans.—The Greeks retire.—Inscription on the rocks.—The commanders of the Persian fleet summoned to Thermopylae.

FROM Therma—the last of the great stations at which the Persian army halted before its final descent upon Greece—the army commenced its march, and the fleet set sail, nearly at the same time, which was early in the summer. The army advanced slowly, meeting with the usual difficulties and delays, but without encountering any special or extraordinary occurrences, until, after having passed through Macedon into Thessaly, and through Thessaly to the northern frontier of Phocis, they began to approach the Straits of Thermopylae. What took place at Thermopylae will be made the subject of the next chapter. The movements of the fleet are to be narrated in this.

In order distinctly to understand these movements, it is necessary that the reader should first have a clear conception of the geographical conformation of the coasts and seas along which the path of the expedition lay. By referring to the map of Greece, we shall see that the course which the fleet would naturally take from Therma to the southeastward, along the coast, was unobstructed and clear for about a hundred miles. We then come to a group of four islands, extending in a range at right angles to the coast. The only one of these islands with which we have particularly to do in this history is the innermost of them, which was named Sciathus. Opposite to these islands the line of the coast, having passed around the point of a mountainous and rocky promontory called Magnesia, turns suddenly to the westward, and runs in that direction for about thirty miles, when it again turns to the southward and eastward as before. In the sort of corner thus cut off by the deflection of the coast lies the long island of Euboea, which may be considered, in fact, as almost a continuation of the continent, as it is a part of the same conformation of country, and is separated from the main land only by submerged valleys on the north and on the east. Into these sunken valleys the sea of course flows, forming straits or channels. The one on the north was, in ancient times, called Artemisium, and the one on the west, at its narrowest point, Euripus. All these islands and coasts were high and picturesque. They were also, in the days of Xerxes, densely populated, and adorned profusely with temples, citadels, and towns.

On passing the southernmost extremity of the island of Euboea, and turning to the westward, we come to a promontory of the main land, which constituted Attica, and in the middle of which the city of Athens was situated. Beyond this is a capacious gulf, called the Saronian Gulf. It lies between Attica and the Peloponnesus. In the middle of the Saronian Gulf lies the island of Ægina, and in the northern part of it the island of Salamis. The progress of the Persian fleet was from Therma down the coast to Sciathus, thence along the shores of Euboea to its southern point, and so round into the Saronian Gulf to the island of Salamis. The distance of this voyage was perhaps two hundred and fifty miles. In accomplishing it the fleet encountered many dangers, and met with a variety of incidents and events, which we shall now proceed to describe.

The country, of course, was every where in a state of the greatest excitement and terror. The immense army was slowly coming down by land, and the fleet, scarcely less terrible, since its descents upon the coast would be so fearfully sudden and overwhelming when they were made, was advancing by sea. The inhabitants of the country were consequently in a state of extreme agitation. The sick and the infirm, who were, of course, utterly helpless in such a danger, exhibited every where the spectacle of silent dismay. Mothers, wives, maidens, and children, on the other hand, were wild with excitement and terror. The men, too full of passion to fear, or too full of pride to allow their fears to be seen, were gathering in arms, or hurrying to and fro with intelligence, or making hasty arrangements to remove their wives and children from the scenes of cruel suffering which were to ensue. They stationed watchmen on the hills to give warning of the approach of the enemy. They agreed upon signals, and raised piles of wood for beacon fires on every commanding elevation along the coast; while all the roads leading from the threatened provinces to other regions more remote from the danger were covered with flying parties, endeavoring to make their escape, and carrying, wearily and in sorrow, whatever they valued most and were most anxious to save. Mothers bore their children, men their gold and silver, and sisters aided their sick or feeble brothers to sustain the toil and terror of the flight.

All this time Xerxes was sitting in his war chariot, in the midst of his advancing army, full of exultation, happiness, and pride at the thoughts of the vast harvest of glory which all this panic and suffering were bringing him in.

The fleet, at length—which was under the command of Xerxes's brothers and cousins, whom he had appointed the admirals of it—began to move down the coast from Therma, with the intention of first sweeping the seas clear of any naval force which the Greeks might have sent forward there to act against them, and then of landing upon some point on the coast, wherever they could do so most advantageously for co-operation with the army on the land. The advance of the ships was necessarily slow. So immense a flotilla could not have been otherwise kept together. The admirals, however, selected ten of the swiftest of the galleys, and, after manning and arming them in the most perfect manner, sent them forward to reconnoiter. The ten galleys were ordered to advance rapidly, but with the greatest circumspection. They were not to incur any needless danger, but, if they met with any detached ships of the enemy, they were to capture them, if possible. They were, moreover, to be constantly on the alert, to observe every thing, and to send back to the fleet all important intelligence which they could obtain.

The ten galleys went on without observing any thing remarkable until they reached the island of Sciathus. Here they came in sight of three Greek ships, a sort of advanced guard, which had been stationed there to watch the movements of the enemy.

The Greek galleys immediately hoisted their anchors and fled; the Persian galleys manned their oars, and pressed on after them.

They overtook one of the guard-ships very soon, and, after a short conflict, they succeeded in capturing it. The Persians made prisoners of the officers and crew, and then, selecting from among them the fairest and most noble-looking man, just as they would have selected a bullock from a herd, they sacrificed him to one of their deities on the prow of the captured ship. This was a religious ceremony, intended to signalize and sanctify their victory.

The second vessel they also overtook and captured. The crew of this ship were easily subdued, as the overwhelming superiority of their enemies appeared to convince them that all resistance was hopeless, and to plunge them into despair. There was one man, however, who, it seems, could not be conquered. He fought like a tiger to the last, and only ceased to deal his furious thrusts and blows at the enemies that surrounded him when, after being entirely covered with wounds, he fell faint and nearly lifeless upon the bloody deck. When the conflict with him was thus ended, the murderous hostility of his enemies seemed suddenly to be changed into pity for his sufferings and admiration of his valor. They gathered around him, bathed and bound up his wounds, gave him cordials, and at length restored him to life. Finally, when the detachment returned to the fleet, some days afterward, they carried this man with them, and presented him to the commanders as a hero worthy of the highest admiration and honor. The rest of the crew were made slaves.

The third of the Greek guard-ships contrived to escape, or, rather, the crew escaped, while the vessel itself was taken. This ship, in its flight, had gone toward the north, and the crew at last succeeded in running it on shore on the coast of Thessaly, so as to escape, themselves, by abandoning the vessel to the enemy. The officers and crew, thus escaping to the shore, went through Thessaly into Greece, spreading the tidings every where that the Persians were at hand. This intelligence was communicated, also, along the coast, by beacon fires which the people of Sciathus built upon the heights of the island as a signal, to give the alarm to the country southward of them, according to the preconcerted plan. The alarm was communicated by other fires built on other heights, and sentinels were stationed on every commanding eminence on the highlands of Euboea toward the south, to watch for the first appearance of the enemy.

The Persian galleys that had been sent forward having taken the three Greek guard-ships, and finding the sea before them now clear of all appearances of an enemy, concluded to return to the fleet with their prizes and their report. They had been directed, when they were dispatched from the fleet, to lay up a monument of stones at the furthest point which they should reach in their cruise: a measure often resorted to in similar cases, by way of furnishing proof that a party thus sent forward have really advanced as far as they pretend on their return. The Persian detachment had actually brought the stones for the erection of their landmark with them in one of their galleys. The galley containing the stones, and two others to aid it, pushed on beyond Sciathus to a small rocky islet standing in a conspicuous position in the sea, and there they built their monument or cairn. The detachment then returned to meet the fleet. The time occupied by this whole expedition was eleven days.

The fleet was, in the mean time, coming down along the coast of Magnesia. The whole company of ships had advanced safely and prosperously thus far, but now a great calamity was about to befall them—the first of the series of disasters by which the expedition was ultimately ruined. It was a storm at sea.

The fleet had drawn up for the night in a long and shallow bay on the coast. There was a rocky promontory at one end of this bay and a cape on the other, with a long beach between them. It was a very good place of refuge and rest for the night in calm weather, but such a bay afforded very little shelter against a tempestuous wind, or even against the surf and swell of the sea, which were sometimes produced by a distant storm. When the fleet entered this bay in the evening, the sea was calm and the sky serene. The commanders expected to remain there for the night, and to proceed on the voyage on the following day.

The bay was not sufficiently extensive to allow of the drawing up of so large a fleet in a single line along the shore. The ships were accordingly arranged in several lines, eight in all. The innermost of these lines was close to the shore; the others were at different distances from it, and every separate ship was held to the place assigned it by its anchors. In this position the fleet passed the night in safety, but before morning there were indications of a storm. The sky looked wild and lurid. A heavy swell came rolling in from the offing. The wind began to rise, and to blow in fitful gusts. Its direction was from the eastward, so that its tendency was to drive the fleet upon the shore. The seamen were anxious and afraid, and the commanders of the several ships began to devise, each for his own vessel, the best means of safety. Some, whose vessels were small, drew them up upon the sand, above the reach of the swell. Others strengthened the anchoring tackle, or added new anchors to those already down. Others raised their anchors altogether, and attempted to row their galleys away, up or down the coast, in hope of finding some better place of shelter. Thus all was excitement and confusion in the fleet, through the eager efforts made by every separate crew to escape the impending danger.

In the mean time, the storm came on apace. The rising and roughening sea made the oars useless, and the wind howled frightfully through the cordage and the rigging. The galleys soon began to be forced away from their moorings. Some were driven upon the beach and dashed to pieces by the waves. Some were wrecked on the rocks at one or the other of the projecting points which bounded the bay on either hand. Some foundered at their place of anchorage. Vast numbers of men were drowned. Those who escaped to the shore were in hourly dread of an attack from the inhabitants of the country. To save themselves, if possible, from this danger, they dragged up the fragments of the wrecked vessels upon the beach, and built a fort with them on the shore. Here they intrenched themselves, and then prepared to defend their lives, armed with the weapons which, like the materials for their fort, were washed up, from time to time, by the sea.

The storm continued for three days. It destroyed about three hundred galleys, besides an immense number of provision transports and other smaller vessels. Great numbers of seamen, also, were drowned.

The inhabitants of the country along the coast enriched themselves with the plunder which they obtained from the wrecks, and from the treasures, and the gold and silver vessels, which continued for some time to be driven up upon the beach by the waves. The Persians themselves recovered, it was said, a great deal of valuable treasure, by employing a certain Greek diver, whom they had in their fleet, to dive for it after the storm was over. This diver, whose name was Scyllias, was famed far and wide for his power of remaining under water. As an instance of what they believed him capable of performing, they said that when, at a certain period subsequent to these transactions, he determined to desert to the Greeks, he accomplished his design by diving into the sea from the deck of a Persian galley, and coming up again in the midst of the Greek fleet, ten miles distant!

After three days the storm subsided. The Persians then repaired the damages which had been sustained, so far as it was now possible to repair them, collected what remained of the fleet, took the shipwrecked mariners from their rude fortification on the beach, and set sail again on their voyage to the southward.

In the mean time, the Greek fleet had assembled in the arm of the sea lying north of Euboea, and between Euboea and the main land. It was an allied fleet, made up of contributions from various states that had finally agreed to come into the confederacy. As is usually the case, however, with allied or confederate forces, they were not well agreed among themselves. The Athenians had furnished far the greater number of ships, and they considered themselves, therefore, entitled to the command; but the other allies were envious and jealous of them on account of that very superiority of wealth and power which enabled them to supply a greater portion of the naval force than the rest. They were willing that one of the Spartans should command, but they would not consent to put themselves under an Athenian. If an Athenian leader were chosen, they would disperse, they said, and the various portions of the fleet return to their respective homes.

The Athenians, though burning with resentment at this unjust declaration, were compelled to submit to the necessity of the case. They could not take the confederates at their word, and allow the fleet to be broken up, for the defense of Athens was the great object for which it was assembled. The other states might make their peace with the conqueror by submission, but the Athenians could not do so. In respect to the rest of Greece, Xerxes wished only for dominion. In respect to Athens, he wished for vengeance. The Athenians had burned the Persian city of Sardis, and he had determined to give himself no rest until he had burned Athens in return.

It was well understood, therefore, that the assembling of the fleet, and giving battle to the Persians where they now were, was a plan adopted mainly for the defense and benefit of the Athenians. The Athenians, accordingly, waived their claim to command, secretly resolving that, when the war was over, they would have their revenge for the insult and injury.

A Spartan was accordingly appointed commander of the fleet. His name was Eurybiades.

Things were in this state when the two fleets came in sight of each other in the strait between the northern end of Euboea and the main land. Fifteen of the Persian galleys, advancing incautiously some miles in front of the rest, came suddenly upon the Greek fleet, and were all captured. The crews were made prisoners and sent into Greece. The remainder of the fleet entered the strait, and anchored at the eastern extremity of it, sheltered by the promontory of Magnesia, which now lay to the north of them.

The Greeks were amazed at the immense magnitude of the Persian fleet, and the first opinion of the commanders was, that it was wholly useless for them to attempt to engage them. A council was convened, and, after a long and anxious debate, they decided that it was best to retire to the southward. The inhabitants of Euboea, who had been already in a state of great excitement and terror at the near approach of so formidable an enemy, were thrown, by this decision of the allies, into a state of absolute dismay. It was abandoning them to irremediable and hopeless destruction.

The government of the island immediately raised a very large sum of money, and went with it to Themistocles, one of the most influential of the Athenian leaders, and offered it to him if he would contrive any way to persuade the commanders of the fleet to remain and give the Persians battle where they were. Themistocles took the money, and agreed to the condition. He went with a small part of it—though this part was a very considerable sum—to Eurybiades, the commander-in-chief, and offered it to him if he would retain the fleet in its present position. There were some other similar offerings made to other influential men, judiciously selected. All this was done in a very private manner, and, of course, Themistocles took care to reserve to himself the lion's share of the Euboean contribution. The effect of this money in altering the opinions of the naval officers was marvelous. A new council was called, the former decision was annulled, and the Greeks determined to give their enemies battle where they were.

The Persians had not been unmindful of the danger that the Greeks might retreat by retiring through the Euripus, and so escape them. In order to prevent this, they secretly sent off a fleet of two hundred of their strongest and fleetest galleys, with orders to sail round Euboea and enter the Euripus from the south, so as to cut off the retreat of the Greeks in that quarter. They thought that by this plan the Greek fleet would be surrounded, and could have no possible mode of escape. They remained, therefore, with the principal fleet, at the outer entrance of the northern strait for some days, before attacking the Greeks, in order to give time for the detachment to pass round the island.

The Persians sent off the two hundred galleys with great secrecy, not desiring that the Greeks should discover their design of thus intercepting their retreat. They did discover it, however, for this was the occasion on which the great diver, Scyllias, made his escape from one fleet to the other by swimming under water ten miles, and he brought the Greeks the tidings.

The Greeks dispatched a small squadron of ships with orders to proceed southward into the Euripus, to meet this detachment which the Persians sent round; and, in the mean time, they determined themselves to attack the main Persian fleet without any delay. Notwithstanding their absurd dissensions and jealousies, and the extent to which the leaders were influenced by intrigues and bribes, the Greeks always evinced an undaunted and indomitable spirit when the day of battle came. It was, moreover, in this case, exceedingly important to defend the position which they had taken. By referring to the map once more, it will be seen that the Euripus was the great highway to Athens by sea, as the pass of Thermopylae was by land. Thermopylae was west of Artemisium, where the fleet was now stationed, and not many miles from it. The Greek army had made its great stand at Thermopylae, and Xerxes was fast coming down the country with all his forces to endeavor to force a passage there. The Persian fleet, in entering Artemisium, was making the same attempt by sea in respect to the narrow passage of Euripus; and for either of the two forces, the fleet or the army, to fail of making good the defense of its position, without a desperate effort to do so, would justly be considered a base betrayal and abandonment of the other.

The Greeks therefore advanced, one morning, to the attack of the Persians, to the utter astonishment of the latter, who believed that their enemies were insane when they thus saw them coming into the jaws, as they thought, of certain destruction. Before night, however, they were to change their opinions in respect to the insanity of their foes. The Greeks pushed boldly on into the midst of the Persian fleet, where they were soon surrounded. They then formed themselves into a circle, with the prows of the vessels outward, and the sterns toward the center within, and fought in this manner with the utmost desperation all the day. With the night a storm came on, or, rather, a series of thundershowers and gusts of wind, so severe that both fleets were glad to retire from the scene of contest. The Persians went back toward the east, the Greeks to the westward, toward Thermopylae—each party busy in repairing their wrecks, taking care of their wounded, and saving their vessels from the tempest. It was a dreadful night. The Persians, particularly, spent it in the midst of scenes of horror. The wind and the current, it seems, set outward, toward the sea, and carried the masses and fragments of the wrecked vessels, and the swollen and ghastly bodies of the dead, in among the Persian fleet, and so choked up the surface of the water that the oars became entangled and useless. The whole mass of seamen in the Persian fleet, during this terrible night, were panic-stricken and filled with horror. The wind, the perpetual thunder, the concussions of the vessels with the wrecks and with one another, and the heavy shocks of the seas, kept them in continual alarm; and the black and inscrutable darkness was rendered the more dreadful, while it prevailed, by the hideous spectacle which, at every flash of lightning, glared brilliantly upon every eye from the wide surface of the sea. The shouts and cries of officers vociferating orders, of wounded men writhing in agony, of watchmen and sentinels in fear of collisions, mingled with the howling wind and roaring seas, created a scene of indescribable terror and confusion.

The violence of the sudden gale was still greater further out at sea, and the detachment of ships which had been sent around Euboea was wholly dispersed and destroyed by it.

The storm was, however, after all, only a series of summer evening showers, such as to the inhabitants of peaceful dwellings on the land have no terror, but only come to clear the sultry atmosphere in the night, and in the morning are gone. When the sun rose, accordingly, upon the Greeks and Persians on the morning after their conflict, the air was calm, the sky serene, and the sea as blue and pure as ever. The bodies and the wrecks had been floated away into the offing. The courage or the ferocity, whichever we choose to call it, of the combatants, returned, and they renewed the conflict. It continued, with varying success, for two more days.

During all this time the inhabitants of the island of Euboea were in the greatest distress and terror. They watched these dreadful conflicts from the heights, uncertain how the struggle would end, but fearing lest their defenders should be beaten, in which case the whole force of the Persian fleet would be landed on their island, to sweep it with pillage and destruction. They soon began to anticipate the worst, and, in preparation for it, they removed their goods—all that could be removed—and drove their cattle down to the southern part of the island, so as to be ready to escape to the main land. The Greek commanders, finding that the fleet would probably be compelled to retreat in the end, sent to them here, recommending that they should kill their cattle and eat them, roasting the flesh at fires which they should kindle on the plain. The cattle could not be transported, they said, across the channel, and it was better that the flying population should be fed, than that the food should fall into Persian hands. If they would dispose of their cattle in this manner, Eurybiades would endeavor, he said, to transport the people themselves and their valuable goods across into Attica.

How many thousand peaceful and happy homes were broken up and destroyed forever by this ruthless invasion!

In the mean time, the Persians, irritated by the obstinate resistance of the Greeks, were, on the fourth day, preparing for some more vigorous measures, when they saw a small boat coming toward the fleet from down the channel. It proved to contain a countryman, who came to tell them that the Greeks had gone away. The whole fleet, he said, had sailed off to the southward, and abandoned those seas altogether. The Persians did not, at first, believe this intelligence. They suspected some ambuscade or stratagem. They advanced slowly and cautiously down the channel. When they had gone half down to Thermopylae, they stopped at a place called Histiaea, where, upon the rocks on the shore, they found an inscription addressed to the Ionians—who, it will be recollected, had been brought by Xerxes as auxiliaries, contrary to the advice of Artabanus—entreating them not to fight against their countrymen. This inscription was written in large and conspicuous characters on the face of the cliff, so that it could be read by the Ionian seamen as they passed in their galleys.

The fleet anchored at Histiaea, the commanders being somewhat uncertain in respect to what it was best to do. Their suspense was very soon relieved by a messenger from Xerxes, who came in a galley up the channel from Thermopylae, with the news that Xerxes had arrived at Thermopylae, had fought a great battle there, defeated the Greeks, and obtained possession of the pass, and that any of the officers of the fleet who chose to do so might come and view the battle ground. This intelligence and invitation produced, throughout the fleet, a scene of the wildest excitement, enthusiasm, and joy. All the boats and smaller vessels of the fleet were put into requisition to carry the officers down. When they arrived at Thermopylae the tidings all proved true. Xerxes was in possession of the pass, and the Greek fleet was gone.

9

The Battle of Thermopylæ

B.C. 480

The pass of Thermopylae.—Its situation.—Ancient intrenchments.—View at Thermopylae.—The allied forces.—Leonidas the Spartan.—Debate in regard to defending Thermopylae.—The decision.—Character of the Spartans.—Their pride.—The Spartans adorn themselves for the battle.—Approach of Xerxes.—The Persian horseman.—His observation.—Report of the horseman.—Conversation with Demaratus.—Xerxes encamps at the pass.—Troops sent into the pass.—Defeat of the Persian detachment.—The Immortals called out.—The Immortals advance to the charge.—Valor of the Greeks.—The Immortals repulsed.—Treachery of Ephialtes.—Joy of Xerxes.—Course of the path.—A Persian detachment sent up the path.—The Phocaeans retreat.—The Greeks surrounded.—Resolution of Leonidas.—Leonidas dismisses the other Greeks.—His noble generosity.—Leonidas retains the Thebans.—Xerxes attacks him.—Terrible combat.—Death of Leonidas.—Stories of the battle.—The two invalids.—Xerxes views the ground.—His treatment of the body of Leonidas.—Message to the fleet.—Xerxes sends for Demaratus.—Conversation with Demaratus.—Plans proposed by him.—Opposition of the admiral.—Decision of Xerxes.

THE pass of Thermopylae was not a ravine among mountains, but a narrow space between mountains and the sea. The mountains landward were steep and inaccessible; the sea was shoal. The passage between them was narrow for many miles along the shore, being narrowest at the ingress and egress. In the middle the space was broader. The place was celebrated for certain warm springs which here issued from the rocks, and which had been used in former times for baths.

The position had been considered, long before Xerxes's day, a very important one in a military point of view, as it was upon the frontier between two Greek states that were frequently at war. One of these states, of course, was Thessaly. The other was Phocis, which lay south of Thessaly. The general boundary between these two states was mountainous, and impassable for troops, so that each could invade the territories of the other only by passing round between the mountains and the shore at Thermopylae.

The Phocaeans, in order to keep the Thessalians out, had, in former times, built a wall across the way, and put up gates there, which they strongly fortified. In order still further to increase the difficulty of forcing a passage, they conducted the water of the warm springs over the ground without the wall, in such a way as to make the surface continually wet and miry. The old wall had now fallen to ruins, but the miry ground remained. The place was solitary and desolate, and overgrown with a confused and wild vegetation. On one side the view extended far and wide over the sea, with the highlands of Euboea in the distance, and on the other dark and inaccessible mountains rose, covered with forests, indented with mysterious and unexplored ravines, and frowning in a wild and gloomy majesty over the narrow passway which crept along the shore below.

The Greeks, when they retired from Thessaly, fell back upon Thermopylae, and established themselves there. They had a force variously estimated, from three to four thousand men. These were from the different states of Greece, some within and some without the Peloponnesus—a few hundred men only being furnished, in general, from each state or kingdom. Each of these bodies of troops had its own officers, though there was one general-in-chief, who commanded the whole. This was Leonidas the Spartan. He had brought with him three hundred Spartans, as the quota furnished by that city. These men he had specially selected himself, one by one, from among the troops of the city, as men on whom he could rely.

It will be seen from the map that Thermopylae is at some distance from the Isthmus of Corinth, and that of the states which would be protected by making a stand at the pass, some were without the isthmus and some within. These states, in sending each a few hundred men only to Thermopylae, did not consider that they were making their full contribution to the army, but only sending forward for the emergency those that could be dispatched at once; and they were all making arrangements to supply more troops as soon as they could be raised and equipped for the service. In the mean time, however, Xerxes and his immense hordes came on faster than they had expected, and the news at length came to Leonidas, in the pass, that the Persians, with one or two millions of men, were at hand, while he had only three or four thousand at Thermopylae to oppose them. The question arose, What was to be done?

Those of the Greeks who came from the Peloponnesus were in favor of abandoning Thermopylae, and falling back to the isthmus. The isthmus, they maintained, was as strong and as favorable a position as the place where they were; and, by the time they had reached it, they would have received great re-enforcements; whereas, with so small a force as they had then at command, it was madness to attempt to resist the Persian millions. This plan, however, was strongly opposed by all those Greeks who represented countries without the Peloponnesus; for, by abandoning Thermopylae, and falling back to the isthmus, their states would be left wholly at the mercy of the enemy. After some consultation and debate, it was decided to remain at Thermopylae. The troops accordingly took up their positions in a deliberate and formal manner, and, intrenching themselves as strongly as possible, began to await the onset of the enemy. Leonidas and his three hundred were foremost in the defile, so as to be the first exposed to the attack. The rest occupied various positions along the passage, except one corps, which was stationed on the mountains above, to guard the pass in that direction. This corps was from Phocis, which, being the state nearest to the scene of conflict, had furnished a larger number of soldiers than any other. Their division numbered a thousand men. These being stationed on the declivity of the mountain, left only two or three thousand in the defile below.

From what has been said of the stern and savage character of the Spartans, one would scarcely expect in them any indications or displays of personal vanity. There was one particular, it seems, however, in regard to which they were vain, and that was in respect to their hair. They wore it very long. In fact, the length of the hair was, in their commonwealth, a mark of distinction between freemen and slaves. All the agricultural and mechanical labors were performed, as has already been stated, by the slaves, a body which constituted, in fact, the mass of the population; and the Spartan freemen, though very stern in their manners, and extremely simple and plain in their habits of life, were, it must be remembered, as proud and lofty in spirit as they were plain and poor. They constituted a military aristocracy, and a military aristocracy is always more proud and overbearing than any other.

It must be understood, therefore, that these Spartan soldiers were entirely above the performance of any useful labors; and while they prized, in character, the savage ferocity of the tiger, they had a taste, in person, for something like his savage beauty too. They were never, moreover, more particular and careful in respect to their personal appearance than when they were going into battle. The field of battle was their particular theater of display, not only of the substantial qualities of strength, fortitude, and valor, but also of such personal adornments as were consistent with the plainness and severity of their attire, and could be appreciated by a taste as rude and savage as theirs. They proceeded, therefore, when established at their post in the throat of the pass, to adorn themselves for the approaching battle.

In the mean time the armies of Xerxes were approaching. Xerxes himself, though he did not think it possible that the Greeks could have a sufficient force to offer him any effectual resistance, thought it probable that they would attempt to make a stand at the pass, and, when he began to draw near to it, he sent forward a horseman to reconnoiter the ground. The horseman rode into the pass a little way, until he came in sight of the enemy. He stopped upon an eminence to survey the scene, being all ready to turn in an instant, and fly at the top of his speed, in case he should be pursued. The Spartans looked upon him as he stood there, but seemed to consider his appearance as a circumstance of no moment, and then went on with their avocations. The horseman found, as he leisurely observed them, that there was an intrenchment thrown across the straits, and that the Spartans were in front of it. There were other forces behind, but these the horseman could not see. The Spartans were engaged, some of them in athletic sports and gymnastic exercises, and the rest in nicely arranging their dress, which was red and showy in color, though simple and plain in form, and in smoothing, adjusting, and curling their hair. In fact, they seemed to be, one and all, preparing for an entertainment.

And yet these men were actually preparing themselves to be slaughtered, to be butchered, one by one, by slow degrees, and in the most horrible and cruel manner; and they knew perfectly well that it was so. The adorning of themselves was for this express and particular end.

The horseman, when he had attentively noticed all that was to be seen, rode slowly back to Xerxes, and reported the result. The king was much amused at hearing such an account from his messenger. He sent for Demaratus, the Spartan refugee, with whom, the reader will recollect, he held a long conversation in respect to the Greeks at the close of the great review at Doriscus. When Demaratus came, Xerxes related to him what the messenger had reported. "The Spartans in the pass," said he, "present, in their encampment, the appearance of being out on a party of pleasure. What does it mean? You will admit now, I suppose, that they do not intend to resist us."

Demaratus shook his head. "Your majesty does not know the Greeks," said he, "and I am very much afraid that, if I state what I know respecting them, I shall offend you. These appearances which your messenger observed indicate to me that the men he saw were a body of Spartans, and that they supposed themselves on the eve of a desperate conflict. Those are the men, practicing athletic feats, and smoothing and adorning their hair, that are the most to be feared of all the soldiers of Greece. If you can conquer them, you will have nothing beyond to fear."

Xerxes thought this opinion of Demaratus extremely absurd. He was convinced that the party in the pass was some small detachment that could not possibly be thinking of serious resistance. They would, he was satisfied, now that they found that the Persians were at hand, immediately retire down the pass, and leave the way clear. He advanced, therefore, up to the entrance of the pass, encamped there, and waited several days for the Greeks to clear the way. The Greeks remained quietly in their places, paying apparently no attention whatever to the impending and threatening presence of their formidable foes.

At length Xerxes concluded that it was time for him to act. On the morning, therefore, of the fifth day, he called out a detachment of his troops, sufficient, as he thought, for the purpose, and sent them down the pass, with orders to seize all the Greeks that were there, and bring them, alive, to him. The detachment that he sent was a body of Medes, who were considered as the best troops in the army, excepting always the Immortals, who, as has been before stated, were entirely superior to the rest. The Medes, however, Xerxes supposed, would find no difficulty in executing his orders.

The detachment marched, accordingly, into the pass. In a few hours a spent and breathless messenger came from them, asking for re-enforcements. The re-enforcements were sent. Toward night a remnant of the whole body came back, faint and exhausted with a long and fruitless combat, and bringing many of their wounded and bleeding comrades with them. The rest they had left dead in the defile.

Xerxes was both astonished and enraged at these results. He determined that this trifling should continue no longer. He ordered the Immortals themselves to be called out on the following morning, and then, placing himself at the head of them, he advanced to the vicinity of the Greek intrenchments. Here he ordered a seat or throne to be placed for him upon an eminence, and, taking his seat upon it, prepared to witness the conflict. The Greeks, in the mean time, calmly arranged themselves on the line which they had undertaken to defend, and awaited the charge. Upon the ground, on every side, were lying the mangled bodies of the Persians slain the day before, some exposed fully to view, ghastly and horrid spectacles, others trampled down and half buried in the mire.

The Immortals advanced to the attack, but they made no impression. Their superior numbers gave them no advantage, on account of the narrowness of the defile. The Greeks stood, each corps at its own assigned station on the line, forming a mass so firm and immovable that the charge of the Persians was arrested on encountering it as by a wall. In fact, as the spears of the Greeks were longer than those of the Persians, and their muscular and athletic strength and skill were greater, it was found that in the desperate conflict which raged, hour after hour, along the line, the Persians were continually falling, while the Greek ranks continued entire. Sometimes the Greeks would retire for a space, falling back with the utmost coolness, regularity, and order; and then, when the Persians pressed on in pursuit, supposing that they were gaining the victory, the Greeks would turn so soon as they found that the ardor of pursuit had thrown the enemies' lines somewhat into confusion, and, presenting the same firm and terrible front as before, would press again upon the offensive, and cut down their enemies with redoubled slaughter. Xerxes, who witnessed all these things from among the group of officers around him upon the eminence, was kept continually in a state of excitement and irritation. Three times he leaped from his throne, with loud exclamations of vexation and rage.

All, however, was of no avail. When night came the Immortals were compelled to withdraw, and leave the Greeks in possession of their intrenchments.

Things continued substantially in this state for one or two days longer, when one morning a Greek countryman appeared at the tent of Xerxes, and asked an audience of the king. He had something, he said, of great importance to communicate to him. The king ordered him to be admitted. The Greek said that his name was Ephialtes, and that he came to inform the king that there was a secret path leading along a wild and hidden chasm in the mountains, by which he could guide a body of Persians to the summit of the hills overhanging the pass at a point below the Greek intrenchment. This point being once attained, it would be easy, Ephialtes said, for the Persian forces to descend into the pass below the Greeks, and thus to surround them and shut them in, and that the conquest of them would then be easy. The path was a secret one, and known to very few. He knew it, however, and was willing to conduct a detachment of troops through it, on condition of receiving a suitable reward.

The king was greatly surprised and delighted at this intelligence. He immediately acceded to Ephialtes's proposals, and organized a strong force to be sent up the path that very night.

On the north of Thermopylae there was a small stream, which came down through a chasm in the mountains to the sea. The path which Ephialtes was to show commenced here, and following the bed of this stream up the chasm, it at length turned to the southward through a succession of wild and trackless ravines, till it came out at last on the declivities of the mountains near the lower part of the pass, at a place where it was possible to descend to the defile below. This was the point which the thousand Phocaeans had been ordered to take possession of and guard, when the plan for the defense of the pass was first organized. They were posted here, not with the idea of repelling any attack from the mountains behind them—for the existence of the path was wholly unknown to them—but only that they might command the defile below, and aid in preventing the Persians from going through, even if those who were in the defile were defeated or slain.

The Persian detachment toiled all night up the steep and dangerous pathway, among rocks, chasms, and precipices, frightful by day, and now made still more frightful by the gloom of the night. They came out at last, in the dawn of the morning, into valleys and glens high up the declivity of the mountain, and in the immediate vicinity of the Phocaean encampment. The Persians were concealed, as they advanced, by the groves and thickets of stunted oaks which grew here, but the morning air was so calm and still, that the Phocaean sentinels heard the noise made by their trampling upon the leaves as they came up the glen. The Phocaeans immediately gave the alarm. Both parties were completely surprised. The Persians had not expected to find a foe at this elevation, and the Greeks who had ascended there had supposed that all beyond and above them was an impassable and trackless desolation.

There was a short conflict, The Phocaeans were driven off their ground. They retreated up the mountain, and toward the southward. The Persians decided not to pursue them. On the other hand, they descended toward the defile, and took up a position on the lower declivities of the mountain, which enabled them to command the pass below; there they paused, and awaited Xerxes's orders.

The Greeks in the defile perceived at once that they were now wholly at the mercy of their enemies. They might yet retreat, it is true, for the Persian detachment had not yet descended to intercept them; but, if they remained where they were, they would, in a few hours, be hemmed in by their foes; and even if they could resist, for a little time, the double onset which would then be made upon them, their supplies would be cut off, and there would be nothing before them but immediate starvation. They held hurried councils to determine what to do.

There is some doubt as to what took place at these councils, though the prevailing testimony is, that Leonidas recommended that they should retire—that is, that all except himself and the three hundred Spartans should do so. "You," said he, addressing the other Greeks, "are at liberty, by your laws, to consider, in such cases as this, the question of expediency, and to withdraw from a position which you have taken, or stand and maintain it, according as you judge best. But by our laws, such a question, in such a case, is not to be entertained. Wherever we are posted, there we stand, come life or death, to the end. We have been sent here from Sparta to defend the pass of Thermopylae. We have received no orders to withdraw. Here, therefore, we must remain; and the Persians, if they go through the pass at all, must go through it over our graves. It is, therefore, your duty to retire. Our duty is here, and we will remain and do it."

After all that may be said of the absurdity and folly of throwing away the lives of three hundred men in a case like this, so utterly and hopelessly desperate, there is still something in the noble generosity with which Leonidas dismissed the other Greeks, and in the undaunted resolution with which he determined himself to maintain his ground, which has always strongly excited the admiration of mankind. It was undoubtedly carrying the point of honor to a wholly unjustifiable extreme, and yet all the world, for the twenty centuries which have intervened since these transactions occurred, while they have unanimously disapproved, in theory, of the course which Leonidas pursued, have none the less unanimously admired and applauded it.

In dismissing the other Greeks, Leonidas retained with him a body of Thebans, whom he suspected of a design of revolting to the enemy. Whether he considered his decision to keep them in the pass equivalent to a sentence of death, and intended it as a punishment for their supposed treason, or only that he wished to secure their continued fidelity by keeping them closely to their duty, does not appear. At all events, he retained them, and dismissed the other allies. Those dismissed retreated to the open country below. The Spartans and the Thebans remained in the pass. There were also, it was said, some other troops, who, not willing to leave the Spartans alone in this danger, chose to remain with them and share their fate. The Thebans remained very unwillingly.

The next morning Xerxes prepared for his final effort. He began by solemn religious services, in the presence of his army, at an early hour; and then, after breakfasting quietly, as usual, and waiting, in fact, until the business part of the day had arrived, he gave orders to advance. His troops found Leonidas and his party not at their intrenchments, as before, but far in advance of them. They had come out and forward into a more open part of the defile, as if to court and anticipate their inevitable and dreaded fate. Here a most terrible combat ensued; one which, for a time, seemed to have no other object than mutual destruction, until at length Leonidas himself fell, and then the contest for the possession of his body superseded the unthinking and desperate struggles of mere hatred and rage. Four times the body, having been taken by the Persians, was retaken by the Greeks: at last the latter retreated, bearing the dead body with them past their intrenchment, until they gained a small eminence in the rear of it, at a point where the pass was wider. Here the few that were still left gathered together. The detachment which Ephialtes had guided were coming up from below. The Spartans were faint and exhausted with their desperate efforts, and were bleeding from the wounds they had received; their swords and spears were broken to pieces, their leader and nearly all their company were slain. But the savage and tiger-like ferocity which animated them continued unabated till the last. They fought with tooth and nail when all other weapons failed them, and bit the dust at last, as they fell, in convulsive and unyielding despair. The struggle did not cease till they were all slain, and every limb of every man ceased to quiver.

There were stories in circulation among mankind after this battle, importing that one or two of the corps escaped the fate of the rest. There were two soldiers, it was said, that had been left in a town near the pass, as invalids, being afflicted with a severe inflammation of the eyes. One of them, when he heard that the Spartans were to be left in the pass, went in, of his own accord, and joined them, choosing to share the fate of his comrades. It was said that he ordered his servant to conduct him to the place. The servant did so, and then fled himself, in great terror. The sick soldier remained and fought with the rest. The other of the invalids was saved, but, on his return to Sparta, he was considered as stained with indelible disgrace for what his countrymen regarded a base dereliction from duty in not sharing his comrade's fate.

There was also a story of another man, who had been sent away on some mission into Thessaly, and who did not return until all was over; and also of two others who had been sent to Sparta, and were returning when they heard of the approaching conflict. One of them hastened into the pass, and was killed with his companions. The other delayed, and was saved. Whether any or all of these rumors were true, is not now certain; there is, however, no doubt that, with at most a few exceptions such as these, the whole three hundred were slain.

The Thebans, early in the conflict, went over in a body to the enemy.

Xerxes came after the battle to view the ground. It was covered with many thousands of dead bodies, nearly all of whom, of course, were Persians. The wall of the intrenchment was broken down, and the breaches in it choked up by the bodies. The morasses made by the water of the springs were trampled into deep mire, and were full of the mutilated forms of men and of broken weapons. When Xerxes came at last to the body of Leonidas, and was told that that was the man who had been the leader of the band, he gloried over it in great exaltation and triumph. At length he ordered the body to be decapitated, and the headless trunk to be nailed to a cross.

Xerxes then commanded that a great hole should be dug, and ordered all the bodies of the Persians that had been killed to be buried in it, except only about a thousand, which he left upon the ground. The object of this was to conceal the extent of the loss which his army had sustained. The more perfectly to accomplish this end, he caused the great grave, when it was filled up, to be strewed over with leaves, so as to cover and conceal all indications of what had been done. This having been carefully effected, he sent the message to the fleet, which was alluded to at the close of the last chapter, inviting the officers to come and view the ground.

The operations of the fleet described in the last chapter, and those of the army narrated in this, took place, it will be remembered, at the same time, and in the same vicinity too; for, by referring to the map, it will appear that Thermopylae was upon the coast, exactly opposite to the channel or arm of the sea lying north of Euboea, where the naval contests had been waged; so that, while Xerxes had been making his desperate efforts to get through the pass, his fleet had been engaged in a similar conflict with the squadrons of the Greeks, directly opposite to him, twenty or thirty miles in the offing.

After the battle of Thermopylae was over, Xerxes sent for Demaratus, and inquired of him how many more such soldiers there were in Greece as Leonidas and his three hundred Spartans. Demaratus replied that he could not say how many precisely there were in Greece, but that there were eight thousand such in Sparta alone. Xerxes then asked the opinion of Demaratus as to the course best to be pursued for making the conquest of the country. This conversation was held in the presence of various nobles and officers, among whom was the admiral of the fleet, who had come, with the various other naval commanders, as was stated in the last chapter, to view the battle-field.

Demaratus said that he did not think that the king could easily get possession of the Peloponnesus by marching to it directly, so formidable would be the opposition that he would encounter at the isthmus. There was, however, he said, an island called Cythera, opposite to the territories of Sparta, and not far from the shore, of which he thought that the king could easily get possession, and which, once fully in his power, might be made the base of future operations for the reduction of the whole peninsula, as bodies of troops could be dispatched from it to the main land in any numbers and at any time. He recommended, therefore, that three hundred ships, with a proper complement of men, should be detached from the fleet, and sent round at once to take possession of that island.

To this plan the admiral of the fleet was totally opposed. It was natural that he should be so, since the detaching of three hundred ships for this enterprise would greatly weaken the force under his command. It would leave the fleet, he told the king, a miserable remnant, not superior to that of the enemy, for they had already lost four hundred ships by storms. He thought it infinitely preferable that the fleet and the army should advance together, the one by sea and the other on the land, and complete their conquests as they went along. He advised the king, too, to beware of Demaratus's advice. He was a Greek, and, as such, his object was, the admiral believed, to betray and ruin the expedition.

After hearing these conflicting opinions, the king decided to follow the admiral's advice. "I will adopt your counsel," said he, "but I will not hear any thing said against Demaratus, for I am convinced that he is a true and faithful friend to me." Saying this, he dismissed the council.

10

The Burning of Athens

B.C. 480

The officers return to their vessels.—The Greek fleet retire to Salamis.—The Thessalians.—Their hostility to the Phocaeans.—Defeat of the Thessalians.—Phocaean stratagem.—A spectral army.—Thessalian cavalry.—Pitfall for the cavalry.—They are caught in it.—Advance of the army.—Cruelties and atrocities.—The sacred town of Delphi.—Mount Parnassus.—Summit of Parnassus.—The Castalian spring.—The oracle.—Architectural structures.—Works of art.—Inspiration of the oracle.—Its discovery.—Panic of the Delphians.—They apply to the oracle.—Response of the oracle.—The prodigy in the temple.—Discomfiture of the Persians.—The spirit warriors.—Consternation at Athens.—The inhabitants advised to fly.—Scenes of misery.—Some of the inhabitants remain.—Situation of the Acropolis.—Magnificent architectural structures.—Statue of Minerva.—The Parthenon.—Xerxes at Athens.—Athens burned.—The citadel taken and fired.—Exaltation of Xerxes.—Messenger sent to Susa.

WHEN the officers of the Persian fleet had satisfied themselves with examining the battle-field at Thermopylae, and had heard the narrations given by the soldiers of the terrible combats that had been fought with the desperate garrison which had been stationed to defend the pass, they went back to their vessels, and prepared to make sail to the southward, in pursuit of the Greek fleet. The Greek fleet had gone to Salamis. The Persians in due time overtook them there, and a great naval conflict occurred, which is known in history as the battle of Salamis, and was one of the most celebrated naval battles of ancient times. An account of this battle will form the subject of the next chapter. In this we are to follow the operations of the army on the land.

As the Pass of Thermopylae was now in Xerxes's possession, the way was open before him to all that portion of the great territory which lay north of the Peloponnesus. Of course, before he could enter the peninsula itself, he must pass the Isthmus of Corinth, where he might, perhaps, encounter some concentrated resistance. North of the isthmus, however, there was no place where the Greeks could make a stand. The country was all open, or, rather, there were a thousand ways open through the various valleys and glens, and along the banks of the rivers. All that was necessary was to procure guides and proceed.

The Thessalians were very ready to furnish guides. They had submitted to Xerxes before the battle of Thermopylae, and they considered themselves, accordingly, as his allies. They had, besides, a special interest in conducting the Persian army, on account of the hostile feelings which they entertained toward the people immediately south of the pass, into whose territories Xerxes would first carry his ravages. This people were the Phocaeans. Their country, as has already been stated, was separated from Thessaly by impassable mountains, except where the Straits of Thermopylae opened a passage; and through this pass both nations had been continually making hostile incursions into the territory of the other for many years before the Persian invasion. The Thessalians had surrendered readily to the summons of Xerxes, while the Phocaeans had determined to resist him, and adhere to the cause of the Greeks in the struggle. They were suspected of having been influenced, in a great measure, in their determination to resist, by the fact that the Thessalians had decided to surrender. They were resolved that they would not, on any account, be upon the same side with their ancient and inveterate foes.

The hostility of the Thessalians to the Phocaeans was equally implacable. At the last incursion which they had made into the Phocaean territory, they had been defeated by means of stratagems in a manner which tended greatly to vex and irritate them. There were two of these stratagems, which were both completely successful, and both of a very extraordinary character.

The first was this. The Thessalians were in the Phocaean country in great force, and the Phocaeans had found themselves utterly unable to expel them. Under these circumstances, a body of the Phocaeans, six hundred in number, one day whitened their faces, their arms and hands, their clothes, and all their weapons, with chalk, and then, at the dead of night—perhaps, however, when the moon was shining—made an onset upon the camp of the enemy. The Thessalian sentinels were terrified and ran away, and the soldiers, awakened from their slumbers by these unearthly-looking troops, screamed with fright, and fled in all directions, in utter confusion and dismay. A night attack is usually a dangerous attempt, even if the assaulting party is the strongest, as, in the darkness and confusion which then prevail, the assailants can not ordinarily distinguish friends from foes, and so are in great danger, amid the tumult and obscurity, of slaying one another. That difficulty was obviated in this case by the strange disguise which the Phocaeans had assumed. They knew that all were Thessalians who were not whitened like themselves. The Thessalians were totally discomfited and dispersed by this encounter.

The other stratagem was of a different character, and was directed against a troop of cavalry. The Thessalian cavalry were renowned throughout the world. The broad plains extending through the heart of their country contained excellent fields for training and exercising such troops, and the mountains which surrounded it furnished grassy slopes and verdant valleys, that supplied excellent pasturage for the rearing of horses. The nation was very strong, therefore, in this species of force, and many of the states and kingdoms of Greece, when planning their means of internal defense, and potentates and conquerors, when going forth on great campaigns, often considered their armies incomplete unless there was included in them a corps of Thessalian cavalry.

A troop of this cavalry had invaded Phocis, and the Phocaeans, conscious of their inability to resist them in open war, contrived to entrap them in the following manner. They dug a long trench in the ground, and then putting in baskets or casks sufficient nearly to fill the space, they spread over the top a thin layer of soil. They then concealed all indications that the ground had been disturbed, by spreading leaves over the surface. The trap being thus prepared, they contrived to entice the Thessalians to the spot by a series of retreats, and at length led them into the pitfall thus provided for them. The substructure of casks was strong enough to sustain the Phocaeans, who went over it as footmen, but was too fragile to bear the weight of the mounted troops. The horses broke through, and the squadron was thrown into such confusion by so unexpected a disaster, that, when the Phocaeans turned and fell upon them, they were easily overcome.

These things had irritated and vexed the Thessalians very much. They were eager for revenge, and they were very ready to guide the armies of Xerxes into the country of their enemies in order to obtain it.

The troops advanced accordingly, awakening every where, as they came on, the greatest consternation and terror among the inhabitants, and producing on all sides scenes of indescribable anguish and suffering. They came into the valley of the Cephisus, a beautiful river flowing through a delightful and fertile region, which contained many cities and towns, and was filled every where with an industrious rural population. Through this scene of peace, and happiness, and plenty, the vast horde of invaders swept on with the destructive force of a tornado. They plundered the towns of every thing which could be carried away, and destroyed what they were compelled to leave behind them. There is a catalogue of twelve cities in this valley which they burned. The inhabitants, too, were treated with the utmost cruelty. Some were seized, and compelled to follow the army as slaves; others were slain; and others still were subjected to nameless cruelties and atrocities, worse sometimes than death. Many of the women, both mothers and maidens, died in consequence of the brutal violence with which the soldiers treated them.

The most remarkable of the transactions connected with Xerxes's advance through the country of Phocis, on his way to Athens, were those connected with his attack upon Delphi. Delphi was a sacred town, the seat of the oracle. It was in the vicinity of Mount Parnassus and of the Castalian spring, places of very great renown in the Greek mythology.

Parnassus was the name of a short mountainous range rather than of a single peak, though the loftiest summit of the range was called Parnassus too. This summit is found, by modern measurement, to be about eight thousand feet high, and it is covered with snow nearly all the year. When bare it consists only of a desolate range of rocks, with mosses and a few Alpine plants growing on the sheltered and sunny sides of them. From the top of Parnassus travelers who now visit it look down upon almost all of Greece as upon a map. The Gulf of Corinth is a silver lake at their feet, and the plains of Thessaly are seen extending far and wide to the northward, with Olympus, Pelion, and Ossa, blue and distant peaks, bounding the view.

Parnassus has, in fact, a double summit, between the peaks of which a sort of ravine commences, which, as it extends down the mountain, becomes a beautiful valley, shaded with rows of trees, and adorned with slopes of verdure and banks of flowers. In a glen connected with this valley there is a fountain of water springing copiously from among the rocks, in a grove of laurels. This fountain gives rise to a stream, which, after bounding over the rocks, and meandering between mossy banks for a long distance down the mountain glens, becomes a quiet lowland stream, and flows gently through a fertile and undulating country to the sea. This fountain was the famous Castalian spring. It was, as the ancient Greek legends said, the favorite resort and residence of Apollo and the Muses, and its waters became, accordingly, the symbol and the emblem of poetical inspiration.

The city of Delphi was built upon the lower declivities of the Parnassian ranges, and yet high above the surrounding country. It was built in the form of an amphitheater, in a sort of lap in the hill where it stood, with steep precipices descending to a great depth on either side. It was thus a position of difficult access, and was considered almost impregnable in respect to its military strength. Besides its natural defenses, it was considered as under the special protection of Apollo.

Delphi was celebrated throughout the world, in ancient times, not only for the oracle itself, but for the magnificence of the architectural structures, the boundless profusion of the works of art, and the immense value of the treasures which, in process of time, had been accumulated there. The various powers and potentates that had resorted to it to obtain the responses of the oracle, had brought rich presents, or made costly contributions in some way, to the service of the shrine. Some had built temples, others had constructed porches or colonnades. Some had adorned the streets of the city with architectural embellishments; others had caused statues to be erected; and others had made splendid donations of vessels of gold and silver, until at length the wealth and magnificence of Delphi was the wonder of the world. All nations resorted to it, some to see its splendors, and others to obtain the counsel and direction of the oracle in emergencies of difficulty or danger.

In the time of Xerxes, Delphi had been for several hundred years in the enjoyment of its fame as a place of divine inspiration. It was said to have been originally discovered in the following manner. Some herdsmen on the mountains, watching their flocks, observed one day a number of goats performing very strange and unaccountable antics among some crevices in the rocks, and, going to the place, they found that a mysterious wind was issuing from the crevices, which produced an extraordinary exhilaration on all who breathed it. Every thing extraordinary was thought, in those days, to be supernatural and divine, and the fame of this discovery was spread every where, the people supposing that the effect produced upon the men and animals by breathing the mysterious air was a divine inspiration. A temple was built over the spot, priests and priestesses were installed, a city began to rise, and in process of time Delphi became the most celebrated oracle in the world; and as the vast treasures which had been accumulated there consisted mainly of gifts and offerings consecrated to a divine and sacred service, they were all understood to be under divine protection. They were defended, it is true, in part by the inaccessibleness of the position of Delphi, and by the artificial fortifications which had been added from time to time to increase the security, but still more by the feeling which every where prevailed, that any violence offered to such a shrine would be punished by the gods as sacrilege. The account of the manner in which Xerxes was repulsed, as related by the ancient historians, is somewhat marvelous. We, however, in this case, as in all others, transmit the story to our readers as the ancient historians give it to us.

The main body of the army pursued its way directly southward toward the city of Athens, which was now the great object at which Xerxes aimed. A large detachment, however, separating from the main body, moved more to the westward, toward Delphi. Their plan was to plunder the temples and the city, and send the treasures to the king. The Delphians, on hearing this, were seized with consternation. They made application themselves to the oracle, to know what they were to do in respect to the sacred treasures. They could not defend them, they said, against such a host, and they inquired whether they should bury them in the earth, or attempt to remove them to some distant place of safety.

The oracle replied that they were to do nothing at all in respect to the sacred treasures. The divinity, it said, was able to protect what was its own. They, on their part, had only to provide for themselves, their wives, and their children.

On hearing this response, the people dismissed all care in respect to the treasures of the temple and of the shrine, and made arrangements for removing their families and their own effects to some place of safety toward the southward. The military force of the city and a small number of the inhabitants alone remained.

When the Persians began to draw near, a prodigy occurred in the temple, which seemed intended to warn the profane invaders away. It seems that there was a suit of arms, of a costly character doubtless, and highly decorated with gold and gems—the present, probably, of some Grecian state or king—which were hung in an inner and sacred apartment of the temple, and which it was sacrilegious for any human hand to touch. These arms were found, on the day when the Persians were approaching, removed to the outward front of the temple. The priest who first observed them was struck with amazement and awe. He spread the intelligence among the soldiers and the people that remained, and the circumstance awakened in them great animation and courage.

Nor were the hopes of divine interposition which this wonder awakened disappointed in the end; for, as soon as the detachment of Persians came near the hill on which Delphi was situated, loud thunder burst from the sky, and a bolt, descending upon the precipices near the town, detached two enormous masses of rock, which rolled down upon the ranks of the invaders. The Delphian soldiers, taking advantage of the scene of panic and confusion which this awful visitation produced, rushed down upon their enemies and completed their discomfiture. They were led on and assisted in this attack by the spirits of two ancient heroes, who had been natives of the country, and to whom two of the temples of Delphi had been consecrated. These spirits appeared in the form of tall and full-armed warriors, who led the attack, and performed prodigies of strength and valor in the onset upon the Persians; and then, when the battle was over, disappeared as mysteriously as they came.

In the mean time the great body of the army of Xerxes, with the monarch at their head, was advancing on Athens. During his advance the city had been in a continual state of panic and confusion. In the first place, when the Greek fleet had concluded to give up the contest in the Artemisian Channel, before the battle of Thermopylae, and had passed around to Salamis, the commanders in the city of Athens had given up the hope of making any effectual defense, and had given orders that the inhabitants should save themselves by seeking a refuge wherever they could find it. This annunciation, of course, filled the city with dismay, and the preparations for a general flight opened every where scenes of terror and distress, of which those who have never witnessed the evacuation of a city by its inhabitants can scarcely conceive.

The immediate object of the general terror was, at this time, the Persian fleet; for the Greek fleet, having determined to abandon the waters on that side of Attica, left the whole coast exposed, and the Persians might be expected at any hour to make a landing within a few miles of the city. Scarcely, however, had the impending of this danger been made known to the city, before the tidings of one still more imminent reached it, in the news that the Pass of Thermopylae had been carried, and that, in addition to the peril with which the Athenians were threatened by the fleet on the side of the sea, the whole Persian army was coming down upon them by land. This fresh alarm greatly increased, of course, the general consternation. All the roads leading from the city toward the south and west were soon covered with parties of wretched fugitives, exhibiting as they pressed forward, weary and wayworn, on their toilsome and almost hopeless flight, every possible phase of misery, destitution, and despair. The army fell back to the isthmus, intending to make a stand, if possible, there, to defend the Peloponnesus. The fugitives made the best of their way to the sea-coast, where they were received on board transport ships sent thither from the fleet, and conveyed, some to Ægina, some to Salamis, and others to other points on the coasts and islands to the south, wherever the terrified exiles thought there was the best prospect of safety.

Some, however, remained at Athens. There was a part of the population who believed that the phrase "wooden walls," used by the oracle, referred, not to the ships of the fleet, but to the wooden palisade around the citadel. They accordingly repaired and strengthened the palisade, and established themselves in the fortress with a small garrison which undertook to defend it.

The citadel of Athens, or the Acropolis, as it was called, was the richest, and most splendid, and magnificent fortress in the world. It was built upon an oblong rocky hill, the sides of which were perpendicular cliffs, except at one end, where alone the summit was accessible. This summit presented an area of an oval form, about a thousand feet in length and five hundred broad, thus containing a space of about ten acres. This area upon the summit, and also the approaches at the western end, were covered with the most grand, imposing, and costly architectural structures that then existed in the whole European world. There were temples, colonnades, gateways, stairways, porticoes, towers, and walls, which, viewed as a whole, presented a most magnificent spectacle, that excited universal admiration, and which, when examined in detail, awakened a greater degree of wonder still by the costliness of the materials, the beauty and perfection of the workmanship, and the richness and profusion of the decorations, which were seen on every hand. The number and variety of statues of bronze and of marble which had been erected in the various temples and upon the different platforms were very great. There was one, a statue of Minerva, which was executed by Phidias, the great Athenian sculptor, after the celebrated battle of Marathon, in the days of Darius, which, with its pedestal, was sixty feet high. It stood on the left of the grand entrance, towering above the buildings in full view from the country below, and leaning upon its long spear like a colossal sentinel on guard. In the distance, on the right, from the same point of view, the great temple called the Parthenon was to be seen, a temple which was, in some respects, the most celebrated in the world. The ruins of these edifices remain to the present day, standing in desolate and solitary grandeur on the rocky hill which they once so richly adorned.

When Xerxes arrived at Athens, he found, of course, no difficulty in obtaining possession of the city itself, since it had been deserted by its inhabitants, and left defenseless. The people that remained had all crowded into the citadel. They had built the wooden palisade across the only approach by which it was possible to get near the gates, and they had collected large stones on the tops of the rocks, to roll down upon their assailants if they should attempt to ascend.

The Citadel at Athens.

Xerxes, after ravaging and burning the town, took up a position upon a hill opposite to the citadel, and there he had engines constructed to throw enormous arrows, on which tow that had been dipped in pitch was wound. This combustible envelopment of the arrows was set on fire before the weapon was discharged, and a shower of the burning missiles thus formed was directed toward the palisade. The wooden walls were soon set on fire by them, and totally consumed. The access to the Acropolis was, however, still difficult, being by a steep acclivity, up which it was very dangerous to ascend so long as the besiegers were ready to roll down rocks upon their assailants from above.

At last, however, after a long conflict and much slaughter, Xerxes succeeded in forcing his way into the citadel. Some of his troops contrived to find a path by which they could climb up to the walls. Here, after a desperate combat with those who were stationed to guard the place, they succeeded in gaining admission, and then opened the gates to their comrades below. The Persian soldiers, exasperated with the resistance which they had encountered, slew the soldiers of the garrison, perpetrated every imaginable violence on the wretched inhabitants who had fled there for shelter, and then plundered the citadel and set it on fire.

The heart of Xerxes was filled with exultation and joy as he thus arrived at the attainment of what had been the chief and prominent object of his campaign. To plunder and destroy the city of Athens had been the great pleasure that he had promised himself in all the mighty preparations that he had made. This result was now realized, and he dispatched a special messenger immediately to Susa with the triumphant tidings.

11

The Battle of Salamis

B.C. 480

Situation of Salamis.—Movements of the fleet and the army.—Policy of the Greeks.—Reasons for retreating to Salamis.—A council of war. —Consultations and debates.—Conflicting views.—The council breaks up in confusion.—Themistocles.—Interview with Mnesiphilus.—Themistocles seeks Eurybiades.—Urges a new council.—The council convened again.—Themistocles rebuked.—Themistocles's arguments for remaining at Salamis.—Fugitives at Salamis.—Views of the Corinthians.— Excitement in the council.—Indignation of Themistocles.—Eurybiades decides to remain at Salamis.—An earthquake.—Advance of the Persians.—Perilous situation of the Greeks.—Xerxes summons a council of war.—Pompous preparations.—Views of the Persian officers.—Views of Queen Artemisia.—Artemisa's arguments against attacking the Greek fleet.—Effect of Artemisia's speech.—Feelings of the council.—Discontent among the Greeks.—Sicinnus.—Bold stratagem of Themistocles.— He sends Sicinnus to the Persians.—Message of Themistocles.—Measures of the Persians.—The Persians take possession of the Psyttalia.— The Greeks hemmed in.—Aristides.—He makes his way through the Persian fleet.—Interview between Aristides and Themistocles.—Their conversation.—Aristides communicates his intelligence to the assembly.— Effect of Aristides intelligence.—Further news.—Adventurous courage of

Paraetius.—Gratitude of the Greeks.—Final preparations for battle.—Friendly offices.—Xerxes's throne.—His scribes.—Summary punishment.—Speech of Themistocles.—He embarks his men.—Excitement and confusion.—Commencement of the battle.—Fury of the conflict.—Modern naval battles.—Observations of Xerxes.—Artemisia.—Enemies of Artemisia.—Her quarrel with Damasithymus.—Stratagem of Artemisia.—She attacks Damasithymus.—Artemisia kills Damasithymus.—Xerxes's opinion of her valor.—Progress of the battle.—The Persians give way.—Heroism of Aristides.—He captures Psyttalia.—The Greeks victorious.—Repairing damages.—Xerxes resolves on flight.—The sea after the battle.—Fulfillment of an ancient prophecy.

SALAMIS is an island of a very irregular form, lying in the Saronian Gulf, north of Ægina, and to the westward of Athens. What was called the Port of Athens was on the shore opposite to Salamis, the city itself being situated on elevated land four or five miles back from the sea. From this port to the bay on the southern side of Salamis, where the Greek fleet was lying, it was only four or five miles more, so that, when Xerxes burned the city, the people on board the galleys in the fleet might easily see the smoke of the conflagration.

The Isthmus of Corinth was west of Salamis, some fifteen miles, across the bay. The army, in retreating from Athens toward the isthmus, would have necessarily to pass round the bay in a course somewhat circuitous, while the fleet, in following them, would pass in a direct line across it. The geographical relations of these places, a knowledge of which is necessary to a full understanding of the operations of the Greek and Persian forces, will be distinctly seen by comparing the above description with the map placed at the commencement of the fifth chapter.

It had been the policy of the Greeks to keep the fleet and army as much as possible together, and thus, during the time in which the troops were attempting a concentration at Thermopylae, the ships made their rendezvous in the Artemisian Strait or Channel, directly opposite to that point of the coast. There they fought, maintaining their position desperately, day after day, as long as Leonidas and his Spartans held their ground on the shore. Their sudden disappearance from those waters, by which the Persians had been so much surprised, was caused by their having received intelligence that the pass had been carried and Leonidas destroyed. They knew then that Athens would be the next point of resistance by the land forces. They therefore fell back to Salamis, or, rather, to the bay lying between Salamis and the Athenian shore, that being the nearest position that they could take to support the operations of the army in their attempts to defend the capital. When, however, the tidings came to them that Athens had fallen, and that what remained of the army had retreated to the isthmus, the question at once arose whether the fleet should retreat too, across the bay, to the isthmus shore, with a view to co-operate more fully with the army in the new position which the latter had taken, or whether it should remain where it was, and defend itself as it best could against the Persian squadrons which would soon be drawing near. The commanders of the fleet held a consultation to consider this question.

In this consultation the Athenian and the Corinthian leaders took different views. In fact, they were very near coming into open collision. Such a difference of opinion, considering the circumstances of the case, was not at all surprising. It might, indeed, have naturally been expected to arise, from the relative situation of the two cities, in respect to the danger which threatened them. If the Greek fleet were to withdraw from Salamis to the isthmus, it might be in a better position to defend Corinth, but it would, by such a movement, be withdrawing from the Athenian territories, and abandoning what remained in Attica wholly to the conqueror. The Athenians were, therefore, in favor of maintaining the position at Salamis, while the Corinthians were disposed to retire to the shores of the isthmus, and co-operate with the army there.

The council was convened to deliberate on this subject before the news arrived of the actual fall of Athens, although, inasmuch as the Persians were advancing into Attica in immense numbers, and there was no Greek force left to defend the city, they considered its fall as all but inevitable. The tidings of the capture and destruction of Athens came while the council was in session. This seemed to determine the question. The Corinthian commanders, and those from the other Peloponnesian cities, declared that it was perfectly absurd to remain any longer at Salamis, in a vain attempt to defend a country already conquered. The council was broken up in confusion, each commander retiring to his own ship, and the Peloponnesians resolving to withdraw on the following morning. Eurybiades, who, it will be recollected, was the commander-in-chief of all the Greek fleet, finding thus that it was impossible any longer to keep the ships together at Salamis, since a part of them would, at all events, withdraw, concluded to yield to the necessity of the case and to conduct the whole fleet to the isthmus. He issued his orders accordingly, and the several commanders repaired to their respective ships to make the preparations. It was night when the council was dismissed, and the fleet was to move in the morning.

One of the most influential and distinguished of the Athenian officers was a general named Themistocles. Very soon after he had returned to his ship from this council, he was visited by another Athenian named Mnesiphilus, who, uneasy and anxious in the momentous crisis, had come in his boat, in the darkness of the night, to Themistocles's ship, to converse with him on the plans of the morrow. Mnesiphilus asked Themistocles what was the decision of the council.

"To abandon Salamis," said Themistocles, "and retire to the isthmus."

"Then," said Mnesiphilus, "we shall never have an opportunity to meet the enemy. I am sure that if we leave this position the fleet will be wholly broken up, and that each portion will go, under its own commander, to defend its own state or seek its own safety, independently of the rest. We shall never be able to concentrate our forces again. The result will be the inevitable dissolution of the fleet as a combined and allied force, in spite of all that Eurybiades or any one else can do to prevent it."

Mnesiphilus urged this danger with so much earnestness and eloquence as to make a very considerable impression on the mind of Themistocles. Themistocles said nothing, but his countenance indicated that he was very strongly inclined to adopt Mnesiphilus's views. Mnesiphilus urged him to go immediately to Eurybiades, and endeavor to induce him to obtain a reversal of the decision of the council. Themistocles, without expressing either assent or dissent, took his boat, and ordered the oarsmen to row him to the galley of Eurybiades. Mnesiphilus, having so far accomplished his object, went away.

Themistocles came in his boat to the side of Eurybiades's galley. He said that he wished to speak with the general on a subject of great importance. Eurybiades, when this was reported to him, sent to invite Themistocles to come on board. Themistocles did so, and he urged upon the general the same arguments that Mnesiphilus had pressed upon him, namely, that if the fleet were once to move from their actual position, the different squadrons would inevitably separate, and could never be assembled again. He urged Eurybiades, therefore, very strenuously to call a new council, with a view of reversing the decision that had been made to retire, and of resolving instead to give battle to the Persians at Salamis.

Eurybiades was persuaded, and immediately took measures for convening the council again. The summons, sent around thus at midnight, calling upon the principal officers of the fleet to repair again in haste to the commander's galley, when they had only a short time before been dismissed from it, produced great excitement. The Corinthians, who had been in favor of the plan of abandoning Salamis, conjectured that the design might be to endeavor to reverse that decision, and they came to the council determined to resist any such attempt, if one should be made.

When the officers had arrived, Themistocles began immediately to open the discussion, before, in fact, Eurybiades had stated why he had called them together. A Corinthian officer interrupted and rebuked him for presuming to speak before his time. Themistocles retorted upon the Corinthian, and continued his harangue. He urged the council to review their former decision, and to determine, after all, to remain at Salamis. He, however, now used different arguments from those which he had employed when speaking to Eurybiades alone; for to have directly charged the officers themselves with the design of which he had accused them to Eurybiades, namely, that of abandoning their allies, and retiring with their respective ships, each to his own coast, in case the position at Salamis were to be given up, would only incense them, and arouse a hostility which would determine them against any thing that he might propose.

He therefore urged the expediency of remaining at Salamis on other grounds. Salamis was a much more advantageous position, he said, than the coast of the isthmus, for a small fleet to occupy in awaiting an attack from a large one. At Salamis they were defended in part by the projections of the land, which protected their flanks, and prevented their being assailed, except in front, and their front they might make a very narrow one. At the isthmus, on the contrary, there was a long, unvaried, and unsheltered coast, with no salient points to give strength or protection to their position there. They could not expect to derive serious advantage from any degree of co-operation with the army on the land which would be practicable at the isthmus, while their situation at sea there would be far more exposed and dangerous than where they then were. Besides, many thousands of the people had fled to Salamis for refuge and protection, and the fleet, by leaving its present position, would be guilty of basely abandoning them all to hopeless destruction, without even making an effort to save them.

This last was, in fact, the great reason why the Athenians were so unwilling to abandon Salamis. The unhappy fugitives with which the island was thronged were their wives and children, and they were extremely unwilling to go away and leave them to so cruel a fate as they knew would await them if the fleet were to be withdrawn. The Corinthians, on the other hand, considered Athens as already lost, and it seemed madness to them to linger uselessly in the vicinity of the ruin which had been made, while there were other states and cities in other quarters of Greece yet to be saved. The Corinthian speaker who had rebuked Themistocles at first, interrupted him again, angrily, before he finished his appeal.

"You have no right to speak," said he. "You have no longer a country. When you cease to represent a power, you have no right to take a part in our councils."

This cruel retort aroused in the mind of Themistocles a strong feeling of indignation and anger against the Corinthian. He loaded his opponent, in return, with bitter reproaches, and said, in conclusion, that as long as the Athenians had two hundred ships in the fleet, they had still a country—one, too, of sufficient importance to the general defense to give them a much better title to be heard in the common consultations than any Corinthian could presume to claim.

Then turning to Eurybiades again, Themistocles implored him to remain at Salamis, and give battle to the Persians there, as that was, he said, the only course by which any hope remained to them of the salvation of Greece. He declared that the Athenian part of the fleet would never go to the isthmus. If the others decided on going there, they, the Athenians, would gather all the fugitives they could from the island of Salamis and from the coasts of Attica, and make the best of their way to Italy, where there was a territory to which they had some claim, and, abandoning Greece forever, they would found a new kingdom there.

Eurybiades, the commander-in-chief, if he was not convinced by the arguments that Themistocles had offered, was alarmed at his declaration that the Athenian ships would abandon the cause of the Greeks if the fleet abandoned Salamis; he accordingly gave his voice very decidedly for remaining where they were. The rest of the officers finally acquiesced in this decision, and the council broke up, the various members of it returning each to his own command. It was now nearly morning. The whole fleet had been, necessarily, during the night in a state of great excitement and suspense, all anxious to learn the result of these deliberations. The awe and solemnity which would, of course, pervade the minds of men at midnight, while such momentous questions were pending, were changed to an appalling sense of terror, toward the dawn, by an earthquake which then took place, and which, as is usually the case with such convulsions, not only shook the land, but was felt by vessels on the sea. The men considered this phenomenon as a solemn warning from heaven, and measures were immediately adopted for appeasing, by certain special sacrifices and ceremonies, the divine displeasure which the shock seemed to portend.

In the mean time, the Persian fleet, which we left, it will be recollected, in the channels between Euboea and the main land, near to Thermopylae, had advanced when they found that the Greeks had left those waters, and, following their enemies to the southward through the channel called the Euripus, had doubled the promontory called Sunium, which is the southern promontory of Attica, and then, moving northward again along the western coast of Attica, had approached Phalerum, which was not far from Salamis. Xerxes, having concluded his operations at Athens, advanced to the same point by land.

The final and complete success of the Persian expedition seemed now almost sure. All the country north of the peninsula had fallen. The Greek army had retreated to the isthmus, having been driven from every other post, and its last forlorn hope of being able to resist the advance of its victorious enemies was depending there. And the commanders of the Persian fleet, having driven the Greek squadrons in the same manner from strait to strait and from sea to sea, saw the discomfited galleys drawn up, in apparently their last place of refuge, in the Bay of Salamis, and only waiting to be captured and destroyed.

In a word, every thing seemed ready for the decisive and final blow, and Xerxes summoned a grand council of war on board one of the vessels of the fleet as soon as he arrived at Phalerum, to decide upon the time and manner of striking it.

The convening of this council was arranged, and the deliberations themselves conducted, with great parade and ceremony. The princes of the various nations represented in the army and in the fleet, and the leading Persian officers and nobles, were summoned to attend it. It was held on board one of the principal galleys, where great preparations had been made for receiving so august an assemblage. A throne was provided for the king, and seats for the various commanders according to their respective ranks, and a conspicuous place was assigned to Artemisia, the Carian queen, who, the reader will perhaps recollect, was described as one of the prominent naval commanders, in the account given of the great review at Doriscus. Mardonius appeared at the council as the king's representative and the conductor of the deliberations, there being required, according to the parliamentary etiquette of those days, in such royal councils as these, a sort of mediator, to stand between the king and his counselors, as if the monarch himself was on too sublime an elevation of dignity and grandeur to be directly addressed even by princes and nobles.

Accordingly, when the council was convened and the time arrived for opening the deliberations, the king directed Mardonius to call upon the commanders present, one by one, for their sentiments on the question whether it were advisable or not to attack the Greek fleet at Salamis. Mardonius did so. They all advised that the attack should be made, urging severally various considerations to enforce their opinions, and all evincing a great deal of zeal and ardor in the cause, and an impatient desire that the great final conflict should come on.

When, however, it came to Artemisia's turn to speak, it appeared that she was of a different sentiment from the rest. She commenced her speech with something like an apology for presuming to give the king her council. She said that, notwithstanding her sex, she had performed her part, with other commanders, in the battles which had already occurred, and that she was, perhaps, entitled accordingly, in the consultations which were held, to express her opinion. "Say, then, to the king," she continued, addressing Mardonius, as all the others had done, "that my judgment is, that we should not attack the Greek fleet at Salamis, but, on the contrary, that we should avoid a battle. It seems to me that we have nothing to gain, but should put a great deal at hazard by a general naval conflict at the present time. The truth is, that the Greeks, always terrible as combatants, are rendered desperate now by the straits to which they are reduced and the losses that they have sustained. The seamen of our fleet are as inferior to them in strength and courage as women are to men. I am sure that it will be a very dangerous thing to encounter them in their present chafed and irritated temper. Whatever others may think, I myself should not dare to answer for the result.

"Besides, situated as they are," continued Artemisia, "a battle is what they must most desire, and, of course, it is adverse to our interest to accord it to them. I have ascertained that they have but a small supply of food, either in their fleet or upon the island of Salamis, while they have, besides their troops, a great multitude of destitute and helpless fugitives to be fed. If we simply leave them to themselves under the blockade in which our position here now places them, they will soon be reduced to great distress. Or, if we withdraw from them, and proceed at once to the Peloponnesus, to co-operate with the army there, we shall avoid all the risk of a battle, and I am sure that the Greek fleet will never dare to follow or to molest us."

The several members of the council listened to this unexpected address of Artemisia with great attention and interest, but with very different feelings. She had many friends among the counselors, and they were anxious and uneasy at hearing her speak in this manner, for they knew very well that it was the king's decided intention that a battle should be fought, and they feared that, by this bold and strenuous opposition to it, Artemisia would incur the mighty monarch's displeasure. There were others who were jealous of the influence which Artemisia enjoyed, and envious of the favor with which they knew that Xerxes regarded her. These men were secretly pleased to hear her uttering sentiments by which they confidently believed that she would excite the anger of the king, and wholly lose her advantageous position. Both the hopes and the fears, however, entertained respectively by the queen's enemies and friends, proved altogether groundless. Xerxes was not displeased. On the contrary, he applauded Artemisia's ingenuity and eloquence in the highest terms, though he said, nevertheless, that he would follow the advice of the other counselors. He dismissed the assembly, and gave orders to prepare for battle.

In the mean time a day or two had passed away, and the Greeks, who had been originally very little inclined to acquiesce in the decision which Eurybiades had made, under the influence of Themistocles, to remain at Salamis and give the Persians battle, became more and more dissatisfied and uneasy as the great crisis drew nigh. In fact, the discontent and disaffection which appeared in certain portions of the fleet became so decided and so open, that Themistocles feared that some of the commanders would actually revolt, and go away with their squadrons in a body, in defiance of the general decision to remain. To prevent such a desertion as this, he contrived the following very desperate stratagem.

He had a slave in his family named Sicinnus, who was an intelligent and educated man, though a slave. In fact, he was the teacher of Themistocles's children. Instances of this kind, in which slaves were refined and cultivated men, were not uncommon in ancient times, as slaves were, in many instances, captives taken in war, who before their captivity had occupied as high social positions as their masters. Themistocles determined to send Sicinnus to the Persian fleet with a message from him, which should induce the Persians themselves to take measures to prevent the dispersion of the Greek fleet. Having given the slave, therefore, his secret instructions, he put him into a boat when night came on, with oarsmen who were directed to row him wherever he should require them to go. The boat pushed off stealthily from Themistocles's galley, and, taking care to keep clear of the Greek ships which lay at anchor near them, went southward toward the Persian fleet. When the boat reached the Persian galleys, Sicinnus asked to see the commander, and, on being admitted to an interview with him, he informed him that he came from Themistocles, who was the leader, he said, of the Athenian portion of the Greek fleet.

"I am charged," he added, "to say to you from Themistocles that he considers the cause of the Greeks as wholly lost, and he is now, accordingly, desirous himself of coming over to the Persian side. This, however, he can not actually and openly do, on account of the situation in which he is placed in respect to the rest of the fleet. He has, however, sent me to inform you that the Greek fleet is in a very disordered and helpless condition, being distracted by the dissensions of the commanders, and the general discouragement and despair of the men; that some divisions are secretly intending to make their escape; and that, if you can prevent this by surrounding them, or by taking such positions as to intercept any who may attempt to withdraw, the whole squadron will inevitably fall into your hands."

Having made this communication, Sicinnus went on board his boat again, and returned to the Greek fleet as secretly and stealthily as he came.

The Persians immediately determined to resort to the measures which Themistocles had recommended to prevent the escape of any part of the Greek fleet. There was a small island between Salamis and the coast of Attica, that is, on the eastern side of Salamis, called Psyttalia, which was in such a position as to command, in a great measure, the channel of water between Salamis and the main land on this side. The Persians sent forward a detachment of galleys to take possession of this island in the night. By this means they hoped to prevent the escape of any part of the Greek squadron in that direction. Besides, they foresaw that in the approaching battle the principal scene of the conflict must be in that vicinity, and that, consequently, the island would become the great resort of the disabled ships and the wounded men, since they would naturally seek refuge on the nearest land. To preoccupy this ground, therefore, seemed an important step. It would enable them, when the terrible conflict should come on, to drive back any wretched refugees who might attempt to escape from destruction by seeking the shore.

By taking possession of this island, and stationing galleys in the vicinity of it, all which was done secretly in the night, the Persians cut off all possibility of escape for the Greeks in that direction. At the same time, they sent another considerable detachment of their fleet to the westward, which was the direction toward the isthmus, ordering the galleys thus sent to station themselves in such a manner as to prevent any portion of the Greek fleet from going round the island of Salamis, and making their escape through the northwestern channel. By this means the Greek fleet was environed on every side—hemmed in, though they were not aware of it, in such a way as to defeat any attempt which any division might make to retire from the scene.

The first intelligence which the Greeks received of their being thus surrounded was from an Athenian general named Aristides, who came one night from the island of Ægina to the Greek fleet, making his way with great difficulty through the lines of Persian galleys. Aristides had been, in the political conflicts which had taken place in former years at Athens, Themistocles's great rival and enemy. He had been defeated in the contests which had taken place, and had been banished from Athens. He now, however, made his way through the enemy's lines, incurring, in doing it, extreme difficulty and danger, in order to inform his countrymen of their peril, and to assist, if possible, in saving them.

When he reached the Greek fleet, the commanders were in council, agitating, in angry and incriminating debates, the perpetually recurring question whether they should retire to the isthmus, or remain where they were. Aristides called Themistocles out of the council. Themistocles was very much surprised at seeing his ancient enemy thus unexpectedly appear. Aristides introduced the conversation by saying that he thought that at such a crisis they ought to lay aside every private animosity, and only emulate each other in the efforts and sacrifices which they could respectively make to defend their country; that he had, accordingly, come from Ægina to join the fleet, with a view of rendering any aid that it might be in his power to afford; that it was now wholly useless to debate the question of retiring to the isthmus, for such a movement was no longer possible. "The fleet is surrounded," said he. "The Persian galleys are stationed on every side. It was with the utmost difficulty that I could make my way through the lines. Even if the whole assembly, and Eurybiades himself, were resolved on withdrawing to the isthmus, the thing could not now be done. Return, therefore, and tell them this, and say that to defend themselves where they are is the only alternative that now remains."

In reply to this communication, Themistocles said that nothing could give him greater pleasure than to learn what Aristides had stated. "The movement which the Persians have made," he said, "was in consequence of a communication which I myself sent to them. I sent it, in order that some of our Greeks, who seem so very reluctant to fight, might be compelled to do so. But you must come yourself into the assembly," he added, "and make your statement directly to the commanders. They will not believe it if they hear it from me. Come in, and state what you have seen."

Aristides accordingly entered the assembly, and informed the officers who were convened that to retire from their present position was no longer possible, since the sea to the west was fully guarded by lines of Persian ships, which had been stationed there to intercept them. He had just come in himself, he said, from Ægina, and had found great difficulty in passing through the lines, though he had only a single small boat, and was favored by the darkness of the night. He was convinced that the Greek fleet was entirely surrounded.

Having said this, Aristides withdrew. Although he could come, as a witness, to give his testimony in respect to facts, he was not entitled to take any part in the deliberations.

The assembly was thrown into a state of the greatest possible excitement by the intelligence which Aristides had communicated. Instead of producing harmony among them, it made the discord more violent and uncontrollable. Of those who had before wished to retire, some were now enraged that they had not been allowed to do so while the opportunity remained; others disbelieved Aristides's statements, and were still eager to go; while the rest, confirmed in their previous determination to remain where they were, rejoiced to find that retreat was no longer possible. The debate was confused and violent. It turned, in a great measure, on the degree of credibility to be attached to the account which

Aristides had given them. Many of the assembly wholly disbelieved it. It was a stratagem, they maintained, contrived by the Athenian party, and those who wished to remain, in order to accomplish their end of keeping the fleet from changing its position.

The doubts, however, which the assembly felt in respect to the truth of Aristides's tidings were soon dispelled by new and incontestable evidence; for, while the debate was going on, it was announced that a large galley—a trireme, as it was called—had come in from the Persian fleet. This galley proved to be a Greek ship from the island of Tenos, one which Xerxes, in prosecution of his plan of compelling those portions of the Grecian territories that he had conquered, or that had surrendered to him, to furnish forces to aid him in subduing the rest, had pressed into his service. The commander of this galley, unwilling to take part against his countrymen in the conflict, had decided to desert the Persian fleet by taking advantage of the night, and to come over to the Greeks. The name of the commander of this trireme was Paraetius. He confirmed fully all that Aristides had said. He assured the Greeks that they were completely surrounded, and that nothing remained for them but to prepare, where they were, to meet the attack which would certainly be made upon them in the morning. The arrival of this trireme was thus of very essential service to the Greeks. It put an end to their discordant debates, and united them, one and all, in the work of making resolute preparations for action. This vessel was also of very essential service in the conflict itself which ensued; and the Greeks were so grateful to Paraetius and to his comrades for the adventurous courage which they displayed in coming over under such circumstances, in such a night, to espouse the cause and to share the dangers of their countrymen, that after the battle they caused all their names to be engraved upon a sacred tripod, made in the most costly manner for the purpose, and then sent the tripod to be deposited at the oracle of Delphi, where it long remained a monument of this example of Delian patriotism and fidelity.

As the morning approached, the preparations were carried forward with ardor and energy, on board both fleets, for the great struggle which was to ensue. Plans were formed; orders were given; arms were examined and placed on the decks of the galleys, where they would be most ready at hand. The officers and soldiers gave mutual charges and instructions to each other in respect to the care of their friends and the disposal of their effects—charges and instructions which each one undertook to execute for his friend in case he should survive him. The commanders endeavored to animate and encourage their men by cheerful looks, and by words of confidence and encouragement. They who felt resolute and strong endeavored to inspirit the weak and irresolute, while those who shrank from the approaching contest, and dreaded the result of it, concealed their fears, and endeavored to appear impatient for the battle.

Xerxes caused an elevated seat or throne to be prepared for himself on an eminence near the shore, upon the main land, in order that he might be a personal witness of the battle. He had a guard and other attendants around him. Among these were a number of scribes or secretaries, who were prepared with writing materials to record the events which might take place, as they occurred, and especially to register the names of those whom Xerxes should see distinguishing themselves by their courage or by their achievements. He justly supposed that these arrangements, the whole fleet being fully informed in regard to them, would animate the several commanders with strong emulation, and excite them to make redoubled exertions to perform their part well. The record which was thus to be kept, under the personal supervision of the sovereign, was with a view to punishments too, as well as to honors and rewards; and it happened in many instances during the battle that ensued, that commanders, who, after losing their ships, escaped to the shore, were brought up before Xerxes's throne, and there expiated their fault or their misfortune, whichever it might have been, by being beheaded on the spot, without mercy. Some of the officers thus executed were Greeks, brutally slaughtered for not being successful in fighting, by compulsion, against their own countrymen.

As the dawn approached, Themistocles called together as many of the Athenian forces as it was possible to convene, assembling them at a place upon the shore of Salamis where he could conveniently address them, and there made a speech to them, as was customary with the Greek commanders before going into battle. He told them that, in such contests as that in which they were about to engage, the result depended, not on the relative numbers of the combatants, but on the resolution and activity which they displayed. He reminded them of the instances in which small bodies of men, firmly banded together by a strict discipline, and animated by courage and energy, had overthrown enemies whose numbers far exceeded their own. The Persians were more numerous, he admitted, than they, but still the Greeks would conquer them. If they faithfully obeyed their orders, and acted strictly and perseveringly in concert, according to the plans formed by the commanders, and displayed the usual courage and resolution of Greeks, he was sure of victory.

As soon as Themistocles had finished his speech, he ordered his men to embark, and the fleet immediately afterward formed itself in battle array.

Notwithstanding the strictness of the order and discipline which generally prevailed in Greek armaments of every kind, there was great excitement and much confusion in the fleet while making all these preparations, and this excitement and confusion increased continually as the morning advanced and the hour for the conflict drew nigh. The passing of boats to and fro, the dashing of the oars, the clangor of the weapons, the vociferations of orders by the officers and of responses by the men, mingled with each other in dreadful turmoil, while all the time the vast squadrons were advancing toward each other, each party of combatants eager to begin the contest. In fact, so full of wild excitement was the scene, that at length the battle was found to be raging on every side, while no one knew or could remember how it began. Some said that a ship, which had been sent away a short time before to Ægina to obtain succors, was returning that morning, and that she commenced

THE HISTORY OF XERXES

the action as she came through the Persian lines. Others said the Greek squadron advanced as soon as they could see, and attacked the Persians; and there were some whose imaginations were so much excited by the scene that they saw a female form portrayed among the dim mists of the morning, that urged the Greeks onward by beckonings and calls. They heard her voice, they said, crying to them, "Come on! come on! this is no time to linger on your oars."

However this may be, the battle was soon furiously raging on every part of the Bay of Salamis, exhibiting a wide-spread scene of conflict, fury, rage, despair, and death, such as had then been seldom witnessed in any naval conflict, and such as human eyes can now never look upon again. In modern warfare the smoke of the guns soon draws an impenetrable veil over the scene of horror, and the perpetual thunder of the artillery overpowers the general din. In a modern battle, therefore, none of the real horrors of the conflict can either be heard or seen by any spectator placed beyond the immediate scene of it. The sights and the sounds are alike buried and concealed beneath the smoke and the noise of the cannonading. There were, however, no such causes in this case to obstruct the observations which Xerxes was making from his throne on the shore. The air was calm, the sky serene, the water was smooth, and the atmosphere was as transparent and clear at the end of the battle as at the beginning. Xerxes could discern every ship, and follow it with his eye in all its motions. He could see who advanced and who retreated. Out of the hundreds of separate conflicts he could choose any one, and watch the progress of it from the commencement to the termination. He could see the combats on the decks, the falling of repulsed assailants into the water, the weapons broken, the wounded carried away, and swimmers struggling like insects on the smooth surface of the sea. He could see the wrecks, too, which were drifted upon the shores, and the captured galleys, which, after those who defended them had been vanquished—some killed, others thrown overboard, and others made prisoners—were slowly towed away by the victors to a place of safety.

There was one incident which occurred in this scene, as Xerxes looked down upon it from the eminence where he sat, which greatly interested and excited him, though he was deceived in respect to the true nature of it. The incident was one of Artemisia's stratagems. It must be premised, in relating the story, that Artemisia was not without enemies among the officers of the Persian fleet. Many of them were envious of the high distinction which she enjoyed, and jealous of the attention which she received from the king, and of the influence which she possessed over him. This feeling showed itself very distinctly at the grand council, when she gave her advice, in connection with that of the other commanders, to the king. Among the most decided of her enemies was a certain captain named Damasithymus. Artemisia had had a special quarrel with him while the fleet was coming through the Hellespont, which, though settled for the time, left the minds of both parties in a state of great hostility toward each other.

It happened, in the course of the battle, that the ship which Artemisia personally commanded and that of Damasithymus were engaged, together with other Persian vessels, in the same part of the bay; and at a time when the ardor and confusion of the conflict was at its height, the galley of Artemisia, and some others that were in company with hers, became separated from the rest, perhaps by the too eager pursuit of an enemy, and as other Greek ships came up suddenly to the assistance of their comrades, the Persian vessels found themselves in great danger, and began to retreat, followed by their enemies. We speak of the retreating galleys as Persian, because they were on the Persian side in the contest, though it happened that they were really ships from Greek nations, which Xerxes had bribed or forced into his service. The Greeks knew them to be enemies, by the Persian flag which they bore.

In the retreat, and while the ships were more or less mingled together in the confusion, Artemisia perceived that the Persian galley nearest her was that of Damasithymus. She immediately caused her own Persian flag to be pulled down, and, resorting to such other artifices as might tend to make her vessel appear to be a Greek galley, she began to act as if she were one of the pursuers instead of one of the pursued. She bore down upon the ship of Damasithymus, saying to her crew that to attack and sink that ship was the only way to save their own lives. They accordingly attacked it with the utmost fury. The Athenian ships which were near, seeing Artemisia's galley thus engaged, supposed that it was one of their own, and pressed on, leaving the vessel of Damasithymus at Artemisia's mercy. It was such mercy as would be expected of a woman who would volunteer to take command of a squadron of ships of war, and go forth on an active campaign to fight for her life among such ferocious tigers as Greek soldiers always were, considering it all an excursion of pleasure. Artemisia killed Damasithymus and all of his crew, and sunk his ship, and then, the crisis of danger being past, she made good her retreat back to the Persian lines. She probably felt no special animosity against the crew of this ill-fated vessel, but she thought it most prudent to leave no man alive to tell the story.

Xerxes watched this transaction from his place on the hill with extreme interest and pleasure. He saw the vessel of Artemisia bearing down upon the other, which last he supposed, of course, from Artemisia's attacking it, was a vessel of the enemy. The only subject of doubt was whether the attacking ship was really that of Artemisia. The officers who stood about Xerxes at the time that the transaction occurred assured him that it was. They knew it well by certain peculiarities in its construction. Xerxes then watched the progress of the contest with the most eager interest, and, when he saw the result of it, he praised Artemisia in the highest terms, saying that the men in his fleet behaved like women, while the only woman in it behaved like a man.

Thus Artemisia's exploit operated like a double stratagem. Both the Greeks and the Persians were deceived, and she gained an advantage by both the deceptions. She saved her life by leading the Greeks to believe that her galley was their friend, and she gained great glory and renown among the Persians by making them believe that the vessel which she sunk was that of an enemy.

Though these and some of the other scenes and incidents which Xerxes witnessed as he looked down upon the battle gave him pleasure, yet the curiosity and interest with which he surveyed the opening of the contest were gradually changed to impatience, vexation, and rage as he saw in its progress that the Greeks were every where gaining the victory. Notwithstanding the discord and animosity which had reigned among the commanders in their councils and debates, the men were united, resolute, and firm when the time arrived for action; and they fought with such desperate courage and activity, and, at the same time, with so much coolness, circumspection, and discipline, that the Persian lines were, before many hours, every where compelled to give way. A striking example of the indomitable and efficient resolution which, on such occasions, always characterized the Greeks, was shown in the conduct of Aristides. The reader will recollect that the Persians, on the night before the battle, had taken possession of the island of Psyttalia—which was near the center of the scene of contest—for the double purpose of enabling themselves to use it as a place of refuge and retreat during the battle, and of preventing their enemies from doing so. Now Aristides had no command. He had been expelled from Athens by the influence of Themistocles and his other enemies. He had come across from Ægina to the fleet at Salamis, alone, to give his countrymen information of the dispositions which the Persians had made for surrounding them. When the battle began, he had been left, it seems, on the shore of Salamis a spectator. There was a small body of troops left there also, as a guard to the shore. In the course of the combat, when Aristides found that the services of this guard were no longer likely to be required where they were, he placed himself at the head of them, obtained possession of boats or a galley, transported the men across the channel, landed them on the island of Psyttalia, conquered the post, and killed every man that the Persians had stationed there.

When the day was spent, and the evening came on, it was found that the result of the battle was a Greek victory, and yet it was not a victory so decisive as to compel the Persians wholly to retire. Vast numbers of the Persian ships were destroyed, but still so many remained, that when at night they drew back from the scene of the conflict, toward their anchorage ground at Phalerum, the Greeks were very willing to leave them unmolested there. The Greeks, in fact, had full employment on the following day in reassembling the scattered remnants of their own fleet, repairing the damages that they had sustained, taking care of their wounded men, and, in a word, attending to the thousand urgent and pressing exigencies always arising in the service of a fleet after a battle, even when it has been victorious in the contest. They did not know in exactly what condition the Persian fleet had been left, nor how far there might be danger of a renewal of the conflict on the following day. They devoted all their time and attention, therefore, to strengthening their defenses and reorganizing the fleet, so as to be ready in case a new assault should be made upon them.

But Xerxes had no intention of any new attack. The loss of this battle gave a final blow to his expectations of being able to carry his conquests in Greece any further. He too, like the Greeks, employed his men in industrious and vigorous efforts to repair the damages which had been done, and to reassemble and reorganize that portion of the fleet which had not been destroyed. While, however, his men were doing this, he was himself revolving in his mind, moodily and despairingly, plans, not for new conflicts, but for the safest and speediest way of making his own personal escape from the dangers around him, back to his home in Susa.

In the mean time, the surface of the sea, far and wide in every direction, was covered with the wrecks, and remnants, and fragments strewed over it by the battle. Dismantled hulks, masses of entangled spars and rigging, broken oars, weapons of every description, and the swollen and ghastly bodies of the dead, floated on the rolling swell of the sea wherever the winds or the currents carried them. At length many of these mournful memorials of the strife found their way across the whole breadth of the Mediterranean, and were driven up upon the beach on the coast of Africa, at a barbarous country called Colias. The savages dragged the fragments up out of the sand to use as fuel for their fires, pleased with their unexpected acquisitions, but wholly ignorant, of course, of the nature of the dreadful tragedy to which their coming was due. The circumstance, however, explained to the Greeks an ancient prophecy which had been uttered long before in Athens, and which the interpreters of such mysteries had never been able to understand. The prophecy was this:

> The Colian dames on Afric's shores
> Shall roast their food with Persian oars.

12

The Return of Xerxes to Persia

B.C. 480

Mardonius.—His apprehensions after the battle.—Depression of Xerxes. —Mardonius's address to him.—Mardonius offers to complete the conquest of Greece.—Effect of Mardonius's address.—Xerxes consults Artemisia.—Artemisia hesitates.—Her advice to Xerxes.—Xerxes adopts Artemesia's advice.—His anxiety increases.—Xerxes commences his retreat.—He sends his family to Ephesus.—Excitement in the Greek fleet.— The Persians pursued.—Debate among the generals.—Themistocles outvoted.—Another stratagem of Themistocles.—His message to Xerxes.— Duplicity of Themistocles.—Retreat of Xerxes.—Horrors of the retreat.— Sufferings from hunger.—Famine and disease.—Xerxes crosses the Hellespont.—Fate of Mardonius.—Xerxes arrives at Susa.—Xerxes's dissolute life.—His three sons.—Artabanus, captain of the guard.—He assassinates Xerxes.—Artaxerxes kills his brother.—He succeeds to the throne.

MARDONIUS, it will be recollected, was the commander-in-chief of the forces of Xerxes, and thus, next to Xerxes himself, he was the officer highest in rank of all those who attended the expedition. He was, in fact, a sort of prime minister, on whom the responsibility for almost all the measures for the government and conduct of the expedition had been thrown. Men in such positions, while they may expect the highest rewards and honors from their sovereign in case of success, have always reason to apprehend the worst of consequences to themselves in case of failure. The night after the battle of Salamis, accordingly, Mardonius was in great fear. He did not distrust the future success of the expedition if it were allowed to go on; but, knowing the character of such despots as those who ruled great nations in that age of the world, he was well aware that he might reasonably expect, at any moment, the appearance of officers sent from Xerxes to cut off his head.

His anxiety was increased by observing that Xerxes seemed very much depressed, and very restless and uneasy, after the battle, as if he were revolving in his mind some extraordinary design. He presently thought that he perceived indications that the king was planning a retreat. Mardonius, after much hesitation, concluded to speak to him, and endeavor to dispel his anxieties and fears, and lead him to take a more favorable view of the prospects of the expedition. He accordingly accosted him on the subject somewhat as follows:

"It is true," said he, "that we were not as successful in the combat yesterday as we desired to be; but this reverse, as well as all the preceding disasters that we have met with, is, after all, of comparatively little moment. Your majesty has gone steadily on, accomplishing most triumphantly all the substantial objects aimed at in undertaking the expedition. Your troops have advanced successfully by land against all opposition. With them you have traversed Thrace, Macedon, and Thessaly. You have fought your way, against the most desperate resistance, through the Pass of Thermopylae. You have overrun all Northern Greece. You have burned Athens. Thus, far from there being any uncertainty or doubt in respect to the success of the expedition, we see that all the great objects which you proposed by it are already accomplished. The fleet, it is true, has now suffered extensive damage; but we must remember that it is upon the army, not upon the fleet, that our hopes and expectations mainly depend. The army is safe; and it can not be possible that the Greeks can hereafter bring any force into the field by which it can be seriously endangered."

By these and similar sentiments, Mardonius endeavored to revive and restore the failing courage and resolution of the king. He found, however, that he met with very partial success. Xerxes was silent, thoughtful, and oppressed apparently with a sense of anxious concern. Mardonius finally proposed that, even if the king should think it best to return himself to Susa, he should not abandon the enterprise of subduing Greece, but that he should leave a portion of the army under his (Mardonius's) charge, and he would undertake, he said, to complete the work which had been so successfully begun. Three hundred thousand men, he was convinced, would be sufficient for the purpose.

This suggestion seems to have made a favorable impression on the mind of Xerxes. He was disposed, in fact, to be pleased with any plan, provided it opened the way for his own escape from the dangers in which he imagined that he was entangled. He said that he would consult some of the other commanders upon the subject. He did so, and then, before coming to a final decision, he determined to confer with Artemisia. He remembered that she had counseled him not to attack the Greeks at Salamis, and, as the result had proved that counsel to be eminently wise, he felt the greater confidence in asking her judgment again.

He accordingly sent for Artemisia, and, directing all the officers, as well as his own attendants, to retire, he held a private consultation with her in respect to his plans.

"Mardonius proposes," said he, "that the expedition should on no account be abandoned in consequence of this disaster, for he says that the fleet is a very unimportant part of our force, and that the army still remains unharmed. He proposes that, if I should decide myself to return to Persia, I should leave three hundred thousand men with him, and he undertakes, if I will do so, to complete, with them, the subjugation of Greece. Tell me what you think of this plan. You evinced so much sagacity in foreseeing the result of this engagement at Salamis, that I particularly wish to know your opinion."

Artemisia, after pausing a little to reflect upon the subject, saying, as she hesitated, that it was rather difficult to decide, under the extraordinary circumstances in which they were placed, what it really was best to do, came at length to the conclusion that it would be wisest for the king to accede to Mardonius's proposal. "Since he offers, of his own accord, to remain and undertake to complete the subjugation of Greece, you can, very safely to yourself, allow him to make the experiment. The great object which was announced as the one which you had chiefly in view in the invasion of Greece, was the burning of Athens. This is already accomplished. You have done, therefore, what you undertook to do, and can, consequently, now return yourself, without dishonor. If Mardonius succeeds in his attempt, the glory of it will redound to you. His victories will be considered as only the successful completion of what you began. On the other hand, if he fails, the disgrace of failure will be his alone, and the injury will be confined to his destruction. In any event, your person, your interests, and your honor are safe, and if Mardonius is willing to take the responsibility and incur the danger involved in the plan that he proposes, I would give him the opportunity."

Xerxes adopted the view of the subject which Artemisia thus presented with the utmost readiness and pleasure. That advice is always very welcome which makes the course that we had previously decided upon as the most agreeable seem the most wise. Xerxes immediately determined on returning to Persia himself, and leaving Mardonius to complete the conquest. In carrying out this design, he concluded to march to the northward by land, accompanied by a large portion of his army and by all his principal officers, until he reached the Hellespont. Then he was to give up to Mardonius the command of such troops as should be selected to remain in Greece, and, crossing the Hellespont, return himself to Persia with the remainder.

If, as is generally the case, it is a panic that causes a flight, a flight, in its turn, always increases a panic. It happened, in accordance with this general law, that, as soon as the thoughts of Xerxes were once turned toward an escape from Greece, his fears increased, and his mind became more and more the prey of a restless uneasiness and anxiety lest he should not be able to effect his escape. He feared that the bridge of boats would have been broken down, and then how would he be able to cross the Hellespont? To prevent the Greek fleet from proceeding to the northward, and thus intercepting his passage by destroying the bridge, he determined to conceal, as long as possible, his own departure. Accordingly, while he was making the most efficient and rapid arrangements on the land for abandoning the whole region, he brought up his fleet by sea, and began to build, by means of the ships, a floating bridge from the main land to the island of Salamis, as if he were intent only on advancing. He continued this work all day, postponing his intended retreat until the night should come, in order to conceal his movements. In the course of the day he placed all his family and family relatives on board of Artemisia's ship, under the charge of a tried and faithful domestic. Artemisia was to convey them, as rapidly as possible, to Ephesus, a strong city in Asia Minor, where Xerxes supposed that they would be safe.

In the night the fleet, in obedience to the orders which Xerxes had given them, abandoned their bridge and all their other undertakings, and set sail. They were to make the best of their way to the Hellespont, and post themselves there to defend the bridge of boats until Xerxes should arrive. On the following morning, accordingly, when the sun rose, the Greeks found, to their utter astonishment, that their enemies were gone.

A scene of the greatest animation and excitement on board the Greek fleet at once ensued. The commanders resolved on an immediate pursuit. The seamen hoisted their sails, raised their anchors, and manned their oars, and the whole squadron was soon in rapid motion. The fleet went as far as to the island of Andros, looking eagerly all around the horizon, in every direction, as they advanced, but no signs of the fugitives were to be seen. The ships then drew up to the shore, and the commanders were convened in an assembly, summoned by Eurybiades, on the land, for consultation.

A debate ensued, in which the eternal enmity and dissension between the Athenian and Peloponnesian Greeks broke out anew. There was, however, now some reason for the disagreement. The Athenian cause was already ruined. Their capital had been burned, their country ravaged, and their wives and children driven forth to exile and misery. Nothing remained now for them but hopes of revenge. They were eager, therefore, to press on, and overtake the Persian galleys in their flight, or, if this could not be done, to reach the Hellespont before Xerxes should arrive there, and intercept his passage by destroying the bridge. This was the policy which Themistocles advocated. Eurybiades, on the other hand, and the Peloponnesian commanders, urged the expediency of not driving the Persians to desperation by harassing them too closely on their retreat. They were formidable enemies after all, and, if they were now disposed to retire and leave the country, it was the true policy of the Greeks to allow them to do so. To destroy the bridge of boats would only be to take effectual measures for keeping the pest among them. Themistocles was outvoted. It was determined best to allow the Persian forces to retire.

Themistocles, when he found that his counsels were overruled, resorted to another of the audacious stratagems that marked his career, which was to send a second pretended message of friendship to the Persian king. He employed the same Sicinnus on this occasion that he had sent before into the Persian fleet, on the eve of the battle of Salamis. A galley was given to Sicinnus, with a select crew of faithful men. They were all put under the most solemn oaths never to divulge to any person, under any circumstances, the nature and object of their commission. With this company, Sicinnus left the fleet secretly in the night, and went to the coast of Attica. Landing here, he left the galley, with the crew in charge of it, upon the shore, and, with one or two select attendants, he made his way to the Persian camp, and desired an interview with the king. On being admitted to an audience, he said to Xerxes that he had been sent to him by Themistocles, whom he represented as altogether the most prominent man among the Greek commanders, to say that the

Greeks had resolved on pressing forward to the Hellespont, to intercept him on his return, but that he, Themistocles, had dissuaded them from it, under the influence of the same friendship for Xerxes which had led him to send a friendly communication to the Persians before the late battle; that, in consequence of the arguments and persuasions of Themistocles, the Greek squadrons would remain where they then were, on the southern coasts, leaving Xerxes to retire without molestation.

All this was false, but Themistocles thought it would serve his purpose well to make the statement; for, in case he should, at any future time, in following the ordinary fate of the bravest and most successful Greek generals, be obliged to fly in exile from his country to save his life, it might be important for him to have a good understanding beforehand with the King of Persia, though a good understanding, founded on pretensions so hypocritical and empty as these, would seem to be worthy of very little reliance. In fact, for a Greek general, discomfited in the councils of his own nation, to turn to the Persian king with such prompt and cool assurance, for the purpose of gaining his friendship by tendering falsehoods so bare and professions so hollow, was an instance of audacious treachery so original and lofty as to be almost sublime.

Xerxes pressed on with the utmost diligence toward the north. The country had been ravaged and exhausted by his march through it in coming down, and now, in returning, he found infinite difficulty in obtaining supplies of food and water for his army. Forty-five days were consumed in getting back to the Hellespont. During all this time the privations and sufferings of the troops increased every day. The soldiers were spent with fatigue, exhausted with hunger, and harassed with incessant apprehensions of attacks from their enemies. Thousands of the sick and wounded that attempted at first to follow the army, gave out by degrees as the columns moved on. Some were left at the encampments; others lay down by the road-sides, in the midst of the day's march, wherever their waning strength finally failed them; and every where broken chariots, dead and dying beasts of burden, and the bodies of soldiers, that lay neglected where they fell, encumbered and choked the way. In a word, all the roads leading toward the northern provinces exhibited in full perfection those awful scenes which usually mark the track of a great army retreating from an invasion.

The men were at length reduced to extreme distress for food. They ate the roots and stems of the herbage, and finally stripped the very bark from the trees and devoured it, in the vain hope that it might afford some nutriment to re-enforce the vital principle, for a little time at least, in the dreadful struggle which it was waging within them. There are certain forms of pestilential disease which, in cases like this, always set in to hasten the work which famine alone would be too slow in performing. Accordingly, as was to have been expected, camp fevers, choleras, and other corrupt and infectious maladies, broke out with great violence as the army advanced along the northern shores of the Ægean Sea; and as every victim to these dreadful and hopeless disorders helped, by his own dissolution, to taint the air for all the rest, the wretched crowd was, in the end, reduced to the last extreme of misery and terror.

At length Xerxes, with a miserable remnant of his troops, arrived at Abydos, on the shores of the Hellespont. He found the bridge broken down. The winds and storms had demolished what the Greeks had determined to spare. The immense structure, which it had cost so much toil and time to rear, had wholly disappeared, leaving no traces of its existence, except the wrecks which lay here and there half buried in the sand along the shore. There were some small boats at hand, and Xerxes, embarking in one of them, with a few attendants in the others, and leaving the exhausted and wretched remnant of his army behind, was rowed across the strait, and landed at last safely again on the Asiatic shores.

The place of his landing was Sestos. From Sestos he went to Sardis, and from Sardis he proceeded, in a short time, to Susa. Mardonius was left in Greece. Mardonius was a general of great military experience and skill, and, when left to himself, he found no great difficulty in re-organizing the army, and in putting it again in an efficient condition. He was not able, however, to accomplish the undertaking which he had engaged to perform. After various adventures, prosperous and adverse, which it would be foreign to our purpose here to detail, he was at last defeated in a great battle, and killed on the field. The Persian army was now obliged to give up the contest, and was expelled from Greece finally and forever.

The Return of Xerxes to Persia.

When Xerxes reached Susa, he felt overjoyed to find himself once more safe, as he thought, in his own palaces. He looked back upon the hardships, exposures, and perils through which he had passed, and, thankful for having so narrowly escaped from them, he determined to encounter no such hazards again. He had had enough of ambition and glory. He was now going to devote himself to ease and pleasure. Such a man would not naturally be expected to be very scrupulous in respect to the means of enjoyment, or to the character of the companions whom he would select to share his pleasures, and the life of the king soon presented one continual scene of dissipation, revelry, and vice. He gave himself up to such prolonged carousals, that one night was sometimes protracted through the following day into another. The administration of his government was left wholly to his ministers, and every personal duty was neglected, that he might give himself to the most abandoned and profligate indulgence of his appetites and passions.

He had three sons who might be considered as heirs to his throne—Darius, Hystaspes, and Artaxerxes. Hystaspes was absent in a neighboring province. The others were at home. He had also a very prominent officer in his court, whose name, Artabanus, was the same with that of the uncle who had so strongly attempted to dissuade him from undertaking the conquest of Greece. Artabanus the uncle disappears finally from view at the time when Xerxes dismissed him to return to Susa at the first crossing of the Hellespont. This second Artabanus was the captain of the king's body-guard and, consequently, the common executioner of the despot's decrees. Being thus established in his palace, surrounded by his family, and protected by Artabanus and his guard, the monarch felt that all his toils and dangers were over, and that there was nothing now before him but a life of ease, of pleasure, and of safety. Instead of this, he was, in fact, in the most imminent danger. Artabanus was already plotting his destruction.

One day, in the midst of one of his carousals, he became angry with his oldest son Darius for some cause, and gave Artabanus an order to kill him. Artabanus neglected to obey this order. The king had been excited with wine when he gave it, and Artabanus supposed that all recollection of the command would pass away from his mind with the excitement that occasioned it. The king did not, however, so readily forget. The next day he demanded why his order had not been obeyed. Artabanus now began to fear for his own safety, and he determined to proceed at once to the execution of a plan which he had long been revolving, of destroying the whole of Xerxes's family, and placing himself on the throne in their stead. He contrived to bring the king's chamberlain into his schemes, and, with the connivance and aid of this officer, he went at night into the king's bed-chamber, and murdered the monarch in his sleep.

Leaving the bloody weapon with which the deed had been perpetrated by the side of the victim, Artabanus went immediately into the bed-chamber of Artaxerxes, the youngest son, and, awaking him suddenly, he told him, with tones of voice and looks expressive of great excitement and alarm, that his father had been killed, and that it was his brother Darius that had killed him. "His motive is," continued Artabanus, "to obtain the throne, and, to make the more sure of an undisturbed possession of it, he is intending to murder you next. Rise, therefore, and defend your life."

Artaxerxes was aroused to a sudden and uncontrollable paroxysm of anger at this intelligence. He seized his weapon, and rushed into the apartment of his innocent brother, and slew him on the spot. Other summary assassinations of a similar kind followed in this complicated tragedy. Among the victims, Artabanus and all his adherents were slain, and at length Artaxerxes took quiet possession of the throne, and reigned in his father's stead.

THE END

ABOUT JACOB ABBOTT

Jacob Abbott was born in Hallowell, Maine in 1803, the son of a minister and farmer. Even as a young boy, he showed academic promise and an interest in spiritual matters. After attending the Hallowell Academy, he was admitted to Bowdoin College at the age of 14.

At Bowdoin, Abbott studied classics and mathematics. He graduated second in his class in 1820 at the young age of 16. He was known as a serious and studious young man who strove for excellence.

After college, Abbott went on to study at Andover Theological Seminary with the intention of becoming a Congregationalist minister. However, his rigorous study habits and frail health caused him to abandon this pursuit after just two years.

Abbott was plagued by gastrointestinal issues and migraines throughout his life, likely exacerbated by the demanding academic environment. His poor health finally forced him to leave his ministerial studies and turn to the less stressful pursuits of writing and tutoring.

First, Abbott took a job as a professor of mathematics and natural philosophy at Amherst College in 1824. The following year, he married Harriet Vaughan and moved to Boston where he opened a school for young ladies. It was during this time that he began writing simple textbooks for teaching science, history and Christian values.

So while Abbott had aspired to be a minister, chronic health issues led him to find an alternate calling educating children through clear and engaging writing. This pivot would launch his successful career as one of the most famous children's authors of the 19th century.

In 1825, Abbott married Harriet Vaughan and soon after started his own school for young ladies in Boston. During this time, he began

ABOUT JACOB ABBOTT

writing educational books in a popular, simple style. His early works included the Mount Vernon Reader and The Young Christian.

Abbott gained fame with the Rollo series, first published in 1835. These stories followed a young boy named Rollo learning morals and virtues through his everyday adventures. The series was hugely popular and established Abbott's reputation as a gifted children's writer.

Other notable books by Abbott include the Franconia Stories (1853-1873), a 10-volume series about a brother and sister's adventures in the country, and the Marco Paul series (1853-1873), which followed a boy's travels around America learning about each state.

In all, Jacob Abbott wrote over 200 books, primarily for young readers. His works were praised for their ability to educate and impart moral lessons in an engaging, story-driven way. Though largely forgotten today, he was one of the most prolific and beloved children's authors of his era.

Abbott continued writing up until his death on October 31, 1879 in Farmington, Maine. His legacy lives on through his contributions to 19th century children's literature.

BIOGRAPHIES ABBOTT WROTE

A number of the books Abbott wrote were biographies of famous people. Famous characters covered in these books included:

Alexander the Great: This book provides a sweeping look at the life and achievements of Alexander III of Macedon, better known as Alexander the Great. It follows his early education by Aristotle, ascension to the throne after his father Philip II's assassination, and extensive military campaigns across Asia and northeast Africa. Abbott recounts Alexander's major battles against the Persians and annexation of their empire. The book also examines Alexander's tactics, military innovations, and creation of a Hellenistic empire stretching from Greece to India before his death at 32.

Alfred the Great: This biography focuses on Alfred's defense of the Kingdom of Wessex against Viking raids in 9th century England. It discusses how Alfred drove back the Great Heathen Army and then negotiated terms with the Vikings, designating parts of England for their settlement. Abbott also highlights Alfred's efforts to revive learning and education in England, as well as his codification of laws and strengthening of the Anglo-Saxon navy. The book frames Alfred as a scholarly, strategic and devout ruler whose achievements laid the foundation for a unified England.

King Charles I: This book looks at the reign of Charles I leading up to and during the English Civil War. It focuses on the religious and political conflicts between Charles I and Parliament, caused largely by

Charles' belief in divine right of kings and many unpopular, authoritarian policies. Abbott also examines Charles' refusal to compromise, leading to the war against Parliament's New Model Army and his eventual execution for treason in 1649 under Oliver Cromwell.

King Charles II: This biography deals with the restoration of the English monarchy under Charles II after the death of Oliver Cromwell. It follows Charles II's return from exile and re-establishment of royal power. However, Abbott also notes Charles' own conflicts with Parliament and religious controversies during his reign. The book discusses Charles' hedonistic lifestyle and many mistresses, but also his support for science, exploration and trade that helped expand the British Empire.

Cleopatra: This book examines Cleopatra VII's life and rule over ancient Egypt. Abbott chronicles Cleopatra's relationships and political alliances with Julius Caesar and Mark Antony, as she sought to maintain Egypt's independence from Rome. The biography highlights Cleopatra's intelligence, education and strategic skills in dealing with Rome. But it ultimately focuses on Cleopatra's downfall and suicide after Mark Antony's defeat by Octavian, leading to Egypt becoming a Roman province.

Cyrus the Great: This biography covers Cyrus II of Persia, founder of the Achaemenid Empire. Abbott traces Cyrus's rise from Persian prince, to revolt against the Medes, to conqueror of the Lydian and Babylonian empires. The book also examines Cyrus's leadership qualities and tolerant policies toward conquered peoples. It portrays Cyrus as a wise, inspirational leader who created the model of a centralized Persian state.

Darius: This book looks at the reign of Darius I, examining his consolidation of the Persian Empire through administrative reforms, development of infrastructure, and expansion of territory. Abbott discusses

Darius's division of the empire into provinces and implementation of a uniform tax system and coinage. The biography also covers his invasion of Greece which was thwarted at the famous Battle of Marathon. Overall, it presents Darius as an capable, pragmatic ruler under whom the Persian Empire reached its zenith.

Queen Elizabeth: This biography celebrates the long and prosperous reign of Queen Elizabeth I of England. Abbott focuses on Elizabeth's shrewd leadership, religious compromise, and patronage of the arts and literature that fostered English Renaissance culture. The book also highlights Elizabeth's naval defeat of the Spanish Armada which secured England's independence from Europe. Overall, Abbott portrays Elizabeth as a commanding, canny and popular female ruler who strengthened England as a major world power.

Genghis Khan: This book looks at the incredible rise of Temüjin, better known as Genghis Khan. It follows his hardships as an outcast youth to becoming the fearsome founder of the Mongol Empire. Abbott chronicles Genghis Khan's brilliant military tactics and utterly ruthless conquests that allowed the Mongols to dominate much of Asia and Eastern Europe. Overall it paints him as a complex figure--strategic genius but also brutal tyrant.

Hannibal: This biography focuses on the great Carthaginian general Hannibal Barca. It recounts his famous crossing of the Alps with war elephants and invasion of Italy during the Second Punic War against Rome. Abbott details Hannibal's victories in major battles like Cannae but also his eventual defeat by Scipio and exile. The book celebrates Hannibal's daring military prowess but also concession late in life that Rome could not be conquered.

Josephine: This book examines the life of Josephine Bonaparte from her aristocratic upbringing in Martinique to her marriage to Napoleon Bonaparte. It focuses on Josephine's time as Empress consort of France and her support for arts and education. But it also discusses Napoleon's eventual divorce from her due to dynastic pressures. Overall the book presents Josephine as an intelligent, compassionate woman who tempered some of Napoleon's ambition.

Julius Caesar: This traces Caesar's life from early military campaigns to dictator and eventual assassination. Abbott covers Caesar's conquest of Gaul, rivalry with Pompey, famously crossing the Rubicon and crowning as dictator. The biography also examines the conspiracy led by Brutus and Cassius to assassinate Caesar in order to save the Roman Republic. In all, the book presents Caesar as an unmatched military mind who irrevocably changed the Roman Empire.

Margaret of Anjou: This biography looks at Margaret of Anjou who became queen consort to England's King Henry VI. It focuses on the political intrigue and machinations Margaret became involved in to support her husband's reign during the War of the Roses. Abbott portrays Margaret as a fiercely devoted, cunning woman who backed the Lancastrians against factions like the Yorkists led by Richard Neville. Though she lost power, the book frames her as a dominant figure during the conflict.

Mary, Queen of Scots: This book examines the life of Mary Stuart who became Queen of Scotland as an infant. It follows her tumultuous reign marked by scandals and plots to overthrow her by Protestants. Her Catholicism also put her at odds with England's Elizabeth I. Abbott recounts Mary's forced abdication, escape to England, and eventual execution ordered by Elizabeth for plotting against her. Overall it presents a tragic figure whose life was marked by political and religious turmoil.

Nero: This biography looks at the notorious Roman emperor Nero. It explores his self-indulgent lifestyle and tyrannical rule marked by possible matricide and the brutal execution of Christians. Abbott also examines legends around Nero like his fiddling during the Great Fire of Rome. The book presents a despotic, unstable man who drastically weakened the Roman Empire.

Peter the Great: This book covers the reforms and policies of Peter the Great that rapidly westernized Russia. Abbott discusses Peter's extensive European travels as a youth and later programs to remake Russia's army, expand its naval fleet, and build a new capital in St. Petersburg. The biography also examines Peter's harsh, authoritarian approach to governing that consolidated his power. Overall it presents him as a pivotal, transformative tsar.

Pyrrhus: This examines the life and military exploits of Pyrrhus, king of Epirus. It focuses on his campaigns against Rome where he won major battles but suffered heavy losses, giving rise to the term "Pyrrhic victory." Abbott recounts Pyrrhus's struggles to build a Greek empire and failed invasion of Sicily against Carthage. Though a skilled commander, Pyrrhus ultimately failed to achieve lasting gains.

Richard I: This biography looks at the reign of Richard I, known as Lionheart. It focuses on Richard's leadership during the Third Crusade to recapture Jerusalem from Saladin. Abbott also details the legendary tales of Richard's bravery and valor in campaigns against France and during his imprisonment. Overall, the book presents Richard I as one of England's great warrior kings.

Richard II: This explores the reign and overthrow of King Richard II. Abbott covers Richard's despotic actions that led the nobles to revolt and install Henry IV, leading to Richard's imprisonment and likely murder. The biography presents a weak king whose tyranny and poor leadership during a peasant's revolt cost him power and his life.

Richard III: This delves into the controversial rule of Richard III. Abbott examines Richard's contested path to the throne and the disappearance of the Princes in the Tower which Richard likely ordered. It also portrays Richard's defeat at the hands of Henry Tudor at the Battle of Bosworth Field that ended the Wars of the Roses. Ultimately Abbott paints Richard III as willing to employ any means to gain and retain the English crown.

Romulus: This recounts the Roman legend of Romulus and Remus, twin brothers raised by a she-wolf who went on to found the city of Rome. Abbott covers the myths of the brothers' quarrel over leadership, with Romulus killing Remus and becoming Rome's first king and architect of its nascent political institutions. Though mythological, Romulus represents ancient Rome's founding origins and rise to power.

William the Conqueror: This biography follows William, Duke of Normandy's conquest of England in 1066 after victory at the Battle of Hastings. Abbott discusses William's reign as king where he consolidated control, introduced feudalism, and fused English and Norman culture. William is presented as a formidable, innovative Norman leader who irrevocably transformed Anglo-Saxon England.

Xerxes: This examines the reign of Xerxes I of Persia, known for his failed invasion of Greece. Abbott focuses on Xerxes's gathering of a massive army to crush Greek resistance, but defeat at Salamis ended his ambitions. The book covers later unrest and palace intrigue that clouded the end of Xerxes's reign. Overall he is portrayed as a rash ruler whose desire for conquest led to disaster for Persia.

www.ingramcontent.com/pod-product-compliance
Lightning Source LLC
Chambersburg PA
CBHW070059080526
44586CB00013B/1120